KV-370-524

Contents

Illustrations

8/10

WG HJ99.   408.

SOLD FROM
REDBRIDGE
PUBLIC LIBRARIES

Highland
Autumn

By W. R. Mitchell

W. R. Mitchell

Highland
Autumn

ROBERT HALE · LONDON

© *W. R. Mitchell 1977*
First published in Great Britain 1977

ISBN 0 7091 6062 3

Robert Hale Limited
Clerkenwell House
Clerkenwell Green
London EC1

LONDON
BOROUGH OF
REDBRIDGE
WITHDRAWN

374.9411

Photoset and bound by Weatherby Woolnough, Northants.
Printed in Great Britain by
Lowe & Brydone Ltd, Thetford.

Between pages 144 and 145

Wet evening at Rannoch Station
A lochan at the edge of Rannoch Moor
Scots pines
A park red stag roaring
Sparring between red stags in a deer park
A red stag and his harem at the time of the rut
A red stag offers a threat display to a rival at the time of the rut
Sir Walter Scott at Loch Katrine
Highland cattle and a deer pony below Ben More
A dead tree on Rannoch Moor

MAPS

(Maps based with permission on the Ordnance Survey)

PICTURE CREDITS

J. Corfield, 2, Arthur Gilpin, 21, Lea MacNally, 34, 35; Tom Parker, 8, 14, 28, 37, 38; The author, 1, 3, 4, 5, 6, 7, 9, 10, 11, 12, 13, 15, 16, 17, 18, 19, 20, 22, 23, 24, 25, 26, 27, 29, 30, 31, 32, 33, 36

For
ROY and KATHLEEN M. ROWLEY

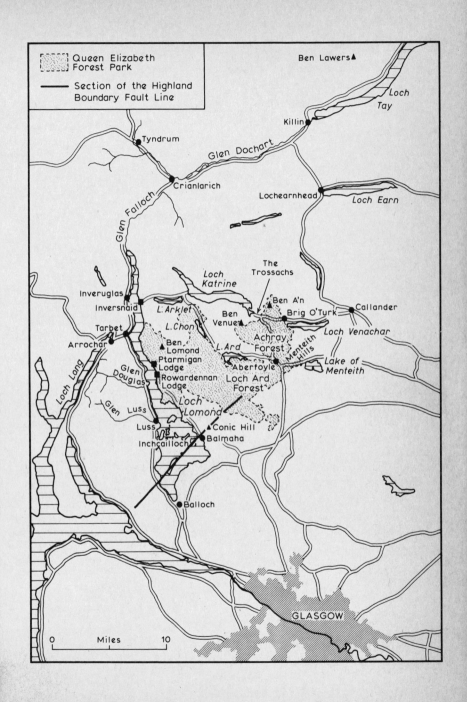

Queen Elizabeth
Forest Park

Section of the Highland
Boundary Fault Line

Ben Lawers▲

Loch Tay

Killin

Tyndrum

Glen Dochart

Crianlarich

Lochearnhead

Loch Earn

Glen Falloch

The Trossachs

Loch Katrine

Ben A'n▲

Inveruglas

Inversnaid

L. Arklet

Ben Venue▲

Brig O'Turk

Callander

L. Chon

Tarbet

Achray Forest

Loch Venachar

Arrochar

Ben Lomond▲
Ptarmigan Lodge

L. Ard

Menteith Hills

Glen Douglas

Rowardennan Lodge

Aberfoyle

Lake of Menteith

Loch Long

Glen Luss

Loch Ard Forest

Loch Lomond

Luss

Conic Hill

Inchcailloch

Balmaha

Balloch

GLASGOW

0   Miles   10

Introduction

Snow and wild geese arrived in Argyll with the September moon. A light snowfall greyed the temples of Ben Cruachan, that amiable giant by the western sea. The geese, vanguard of flocks from Iceland, flew in wavering lines over the mouth of Loch Etive. Later, more geese wiffled above the great marsh at Crinan.

My Highland autumn began with the cries of bird refugees from the northlands – with skeins of grey geese crossing the sky as wideflung chevrons or, in their ponderous manoeuvring, looking like dark beads strung between the clouds.

I watched the passing squadrons from a friend's house at Kinnoull, on the hill above Perth. These geese had used the central route, high over Drumochter and Dunkeld. They progressed across a pearl-grey sky in their thousands; they descended to the valley of the Tay, where their sombre ranks were clearly visible against the pale stubbles. These birds would later move to the 'tatie' fields, and by November over a third of the pink-footed geese wintering in Britain would be marshalled on the big fields within a score of miles of Perth.

White-fronted geese from colonies on the west coast of Greenland appeared at traditional wintering grounds on the isle of Islay, by Loch Ken, and, in smaller numbers, where the Endrick flows into Loch Lomond. And as an autumn wind stirred the lochans and drew a comb through tinted vegetation, I heard the double bugle call of the whooper swan. Family parties of swans cruised with necks straight as brush-shafts and tails at a jaunty angle. The young of the year were distinguishable from the adults since they were garbed in grey and had white on their mandibles. Forty years ago, Seton Gordon photographed nesting whoopers in Argyll.

I was always conscious of bird-life on the move. Fieldfares and redwings from Scandinavia led a nomadic life, stopping for a while where food was plentiful. On a still evening I was over-taken by a flock of golden plover and actually heard their angled wings rustling. Small wading birds that nested on the tundra, and were now in their greyish winter garb, scuttered beside the sea lochs like restless mice.

I was to recall the wild geese most vividly. Snow, geese and Scotland have for long been interconnected in my mind. A Pennine farmer, seeing the first hard flakes of snow swirling just before Christmas, used to chant: "They're pluckin' geese in Scotland, an' sending t'feathers here." As *he* plucked geese, ripping off the tough outer feathers, then stripping away an insulating coat of down, he would add: "A goose doesn't feel t'cold, tha knaws – it wears a jacket and a waistcoat."

I donned a jumper, if not a waistcoat, on seeing snow-crusted Ben Cruachan. I asked a stalker if, somehow, autumn had been overlooked that year. Had the seasons switched directly from summer to winter? "Och, no," was his simple reply. He was very thrifty with words and, as yet, had not sized me up.

The hills were temporarily frozen, but mild air wafted the western glens and sea lochs. The wind dropped each evening. Frost stung hard at night, yet the reappearance of the sun next morning soon warmed the district.

Ben Cruachan, which I viewed from every angle during my Highland jaunt, stands four-square to the weather on a base with a circumference of some twenty miles. Its name should most properly be rendered Cruachan Ben, but I fell in with the local way of putting Ben first! It looked sublime at night, when its slopes were silvered by snow, frost and moonlight. At times, indeed, it resembled a piece of stage scenery – an extravagance intended for a Wagnerian opera. Ben Cruachan became my favourite view and (when I felt energetic) my preferred view-point.

Viewed from one direction, the hill showed a single spire. Seen from another direction, it had two prominent peaks, like those of supporting poles within a flopping ridge tent, each 'pole' exceeding 3,600 feet. I watched the Ben shedding its morning mist and colouring up with a new day. I saw the hill standing blue-black under cloud when all around was sunlit. I would sit up in bed at my lodgings in Taynuilt and glance through the window to see the hill, a silvery form against a sky that looked like black velvet. At breakfast, I again glanced at Cruachan as the sun heaved itself above one of its broad shoulders ready to banish a few wraiths that wandered round the hill like lost spirits.

The stalker who was taciturn when first addressed now become quite a chatterbox. The whole year had been "gey queer", he said. In sultry January, the farmers had worked without jackets. Winter had a sting in its tail, bombarding the Cairngorms with hail and snow in June and sending early tourists dashing for the suntraps of the far west. One week began with snow and ended with unremitting heat in which red deer in Central Scotland crowded the isolated patches of snow to keep cool. High summer was, as usual, rather dull and wet, the stalker added.

We rejoiced at a change of the weather. The wind veered to the north and moderated, becalming a few cumulus clouds. Hills that had been squelchy underfoot, wrapped in cloud, were now sharply delineated. The rain had come close to ruining the hay crop, and I saw a few stooks of corn – the last of the harvest – lolling damply at farms between Etive and Glencoe. Each stook wore a protective bonnet made from plastic sheeting or old fertilizer bags.

The sky had not quite run out of rain. In the late afternoon, a wind would stir the air, mustering a few dark clouds off the coast; the clouds drifted inland, trailing sheets of vapour in which glowed the stub-ends of rainbows. It was easy to dodge the showers.

In Argyll, I had entered a region where I, a stranger, had difficulty in pronouncing place-names. An eleven-year-old schoolboy who was learning Gaelic at Oban was my interpreter, and we pored over the maps in the evening. Names like Buchaille Etive Mor and Buchaille Etive Beag – which I pronounced haltingly – fell like music from his tongue. (He patiently explained that they meant, simply, the big and little herdsmen of Etive.) Looking back, I remember particularly that boy's patience with an ignorant adult! Ranging across the map, we found that Gaelic words for birch, dog and waterfall were incorporated in the names of fields in Glencoe.

Was it fancy, or did I detect – during those pleasant meanderings across the Ordnance Survey – a faint flavour of Old Ireland, a lingering echo of the times when settlers from Dalriada, in Northern Ireland, arrived in Islay and Kintyre and then crossed to the mainland? The very name 'Argyll' means 'coastline of the Gael'.

Scottish history demands the specialist's touch. I was content to know that I travelled through Campbell country. In the mid-eighteenth century, this powerful and numerically strong clan spread itself over a tract of country 100 miles long and some 80 miles wide. At Inveraray, historic capital of Argyll, I dutifully walked up to the castle to tour its main rooms – rooms that, a few months later, were gutted by fire. Someone showed me a copy of *The Oban Times*, with its full coverage of the Argyllshire Gathering, held in town a few days before. On the front page was a photograph that accentuated the Scottishness of the occasion – of stewards on a traditional march to the games field, each clad in full Highland dress. Among the celebrities to be seen was the Duke of Argyll.

The natural scene was my main interest. As autumn came to the west, bracken on the lower hills died back with a spectacular show of tints. Stevenson wrote of "vacant wine-red moor", but the heather blossom was fading. Bracken gave radiance to the autumn, its tall fronds flopping in tangled heaps that were tinted copper and yellow. There were coppery patches on the open hills where deer grass was in decline.

The tinted leaves of rowan enlivened many a ravine and gave a splash of regal colours to the environs of the farmsteads, some of them ruined, alas. Rowan berries became orange-red in late summer. Even before this fruit was fully ripe, the thrushes gobbled it with the gusto of small boys at a party. To the Norse settlers of over 1,000 years ago, the rowan was *raun*, and a Highlander would plant one or two trees near his home to discourage witches.

All the fruit-bearing trees were being ravaged by birds, some of which had by now taken a long southerly journey to their wintering grounds. Ring ouzels, having feasted on rowan and thorn, slipped off under cover of darkness to their winter quarters on the Atlas Mountains of North America. At least, we presume they go by darkness; few birds are seen on migration by day.

A ready-made and bountiful banquet of bright fruit now attracted immigrants from Scandinavia – the fieldfares and red-wings. Not until the hillside trees had been stripped did they descend to the glens. The frosty voices of fieldfares cut into the stillness of autumn afternoons by Loch Lomond. When the birds pitched down in a field, they displayed slate-grey patches on head, nape and rump.

Trees cut their losses and jettisoned leaves. The deciduous woods held a rich show of tints, and further beauty was revealed when the autumn sunshine, intense like a searchlight, illuminated the woodland litter. One morning, rising before dawn to be in position for deer-watching at first light, I saw there had been a heavy fall of leaves during the night. Nothing had disturbed those leaves until the tyres of my car crunched many of them flat against the tarmac. I remember the swish of the leaves and their crisp beauty revealed by the headlamp beams.

Birches, having cast their brown-winged seeds to the wind, now stood primly with arms full of shimmering golden leaves. The 'birks' of high ground were the first to reveal their autumn tints. Bracket fungi jutting from the silver and black trunks were like small ledges, though some specimens were almost the size of dinner plates. Alders, standing in the cool dampness of the burnsides, would broadcast seeds that have the happy facility of being able to float.

The dark, drool pine enhanced every setting. It did not have a conspicuous autumnal show, but responded with a glow of orange to the hard evening sunlight, each pine being topped off with bottle-green foliage.

In my journey west, I saw a succession of hill ridges and lochs. No day in Argyll lacks brightness because this is, overall, a region of shining water; early travellers were as familiar with a boat as with a horse. So extensive were some of the lochs that I was uncertain, when standing beside them, if the water would be clear or salt to the taste.

Loch Fyne extends from the open sea for about eighty miles. As I stood on the pier at Inveraray, the seaside was out of mind until an angler landed a mackerel, and his neighbour gave a whoop when a codling came to the bait. A third angler pointed out jellyfish in full sail; I watched them wreck themselves on the beach, where they soon became uninteresting transparent lumps. Then some herring gulls wailed, and eider ducks cruised by, seeking out the mussel beds. Basking sharks – inoffensive giants – had been seen by watchers on this very pier earlier in the year.

The sights of early autumn included drifts of the Grass of Parnassus, also scabious in upper Glen Shira. Here, too, were the flickering forms of butterflies – red admiral, meadow brown, peacock.

October was the "month of the roaring". The red stags were amorous. Every impression of the Highlands, in prose or verse, should include a deer. Impressions recorded in verse include these lines which have the power to make the Highlander weep with emotion:

> My heart's in the Highlands, my heart is not here;
> My heart's in the Highlands a-hunting the deer;
> A chasing the wild deer, and following the roe,
> My heart's in the Highlands wherever I go.

There was excitement in the air with the fading of daylight. Then the hills were alive with the sound of roaring. I watched a large hill stag, black and fearsome-looking after wallowing in liquid peat, lumber off to rejoin a group of hinds at the feeding grounds. I saw him lift his head, and noticed a dirt-matted mane that gave him a ragged appearance. The stag opened his mouth until the gap was a dark O and he gave a deep, throaty call. It was not vibrant, not especially loud, but it seemed to carry far over the otherwise silent hill: a sound that has made the Highland air tremble since long before man shuffled on to the scene.

A Forestry Commission worker who was ploughing a lonely hillside in advance of tree-planting found the red deer rut exciting. Each morning he walked up the hill to where he left his caterpillar-tracked machine and plough. Several times he came face to face with the local master stag, and he sometimes wondered whether to smile at it or take to his heels. The forester would have the last laugh. Soon a stretch of fencing would deny the deer access to this part of the hill, which would then acquire a blanket of spruce.

It had been a grim year for deer. Not until June did grass contain enough sap to make the hill ends green. In June I saw evidence of the heavy springtime mortality – deer skeletons, to which dense winter hair clung patchily. Scavengers had stripped the bodies of flesh, and in one case cotton grass was growing between the bleached bones. In an ensuing heatwave, large areas of hill were scorched and the burns lost their voices. Groups of deer, deprived of real nourishment, appeared on low ground long before the usual season.

In contrast, roe deer have slipped inconspicuously through the Highland years. Argyll has a high density of roe. At the time of my visit, the bucks were reclusive, recovering from the excesses of the rut, a summertime event. Does and their offspring appeared from woodland cover at dusk. Down in Kintyre, sika stags advertised their presence to the hinds at dusk with a squealing of nasal origin that sounded like whistling if heard from a distance. Like the red stags, the sika wallowed in peaty pools from which they emerged dark and dripping.

A disadvantage of touring in autumn comes from the shortening days. Light fades at about 7 p.m., unless one happens to be near the sea, where a sunset can turn the water pink or even – as I saw from Oban – an outrageous red, prolonging the period during which observation in detail was possible. Yet autumn was the season chosen for Highland travel by the well-to-do of the nineteenth century. Long before the establishment of a Highland Tourist Board, groups of visitors used this period between midge-time and snow-time for their north-country wanderings. Among them was Queen Victoria, she who became the arbiter of what was considered to be good Highland taste. As summer waned, no one could persuade her to stay in London. A trickle of eager sightseers became a flood as new roads were built in the glens and, in due course, Victoria put the royal mark of approval on a Highland jaunt.

She and her consort were at Taymouth Castle, near Loch Tay, in 1842, and the days were spent pleasantly in admiration of the views; they also watched piping and parades by kilted men. Five years later, the royal party visited the west. In the wet!

The royal yacht dawdled on its way up the west coast. The Queen expressed a wish to see Fingal's Cave, and so the vessel was directed round Mull to Staffa and then Iona. In due course, the yacht was tied up at Fort William, from where the visitors travelled by carriage to Ardverikie by Loch Laggan. Victoria was truly in love with the Highlands, for she spoke well of them despite frequent soakings. At Ardverikie, Albert went off north-wards to keep a previous appointment, and his wife remained staring through misted windows on a scene in which sky and land had apparently become one. The countryside was fine, she wrote, "but the weather was most dreadful".

Rain descended on the carriages during the return to Fort William, and the royal yacht slammed through heavy seas. "I was very ill," wrote the Queen. "Albert, however, stood it perfectly, and the children very tolerably." Later, hearing that the eastern part of Scotland had enjoyed pleasant and sunny weather, the royal couple established their Highland home at Balmoral on Deeside.

The tour of 1847 – and, more precisely, the publication of the Queen's Highland journal – created a tourist boom that was aided, in due course, by the establishment of railheads at Oban (1880), Kyle of Lochalsh (1897) and Mallaig (1901).

My jaunt was stimulated by the writing of Dorothy Words-worth. Over forty years before the Royal Soaking at Ardverikie, William and Dorothy, of Grasmere, toured parts of the west Highlands, initially in the company of their friend Coleridge. In 1803, the autumn weather alternated between wet spells and periods that were sharp and cold. After traversing Glencoe, Dorothy wrote in her journal: "The sun was now setting, the air very cold, the sky clear; I could have fancied it was winter-time, with hard frost." Dorothy, the romantic, offered us word pictures of distinction – descriptions of bare hills, floating mists, scattered stones, herds of black cattle. Being unfamiliar with Scotland, she found novelty in every facet of its life and landform.

They travelled in a horse-drawn vehicle, but frequently took to their feet to explore the hills, or were rowed across the lochs. Their visit to the Trossachs was a combination of hill-walking and boating. William, who had visited the country briefly in the autumn of 1801, was anxious to see again the "shot-silk finery" of the autumn purple on the hills. Mary Wordsworth, his wife, was left at Grasmere – holding a new baby!

The English trio crossed the Highland line while travelling by Loch Lomond, and William – fresh from his more intimate

Cumbrian landscape – was at first depressed by the considerable height of the hills and the length of the lochs. West Highland weather was a regular concern. Dorothy, staying at Tarbet, wrote: "Having heard so much of the long rains since we came to Scotland, we had no hope that it would be over in less than three weeks at the least."

It was while re-reading Dorothy's perceptive journal that I decided to follow their route and also to savour the delights of a Highland autumn. I would travel by Lochs Fyne, Awe and Etive; on through Appin and Glencoe; back over the Black Mount and, while staying in the vicinity of Loch Lomond, venture into the Trossachs.

The Wordsworths, accustomed to High Thinking and Spartan Living, were nonetheless surprised by the poverty of Highland folk and startled by the primitive nature of the accommodation. They stayed at the King's House, near the head of Glencoe, "a large square building, cased in blue slates to defend it from storms". Entering, they saw two sheep hung up, "as if just killed from the barren moor, their bones hardly sheathed in flesh". The shoulder of mutton provided at mealtime was so hard it was "impossible to chew the little flesh that might be scraped off the bones". The fire was sustained by wet peats. William had to guard his horse from the attention of other horses as it ate the corn provided, "or it would have been robbed of its meal by others standing like wild beasts to devour each other's portion". The bed sheets were damp!

Earlier, at Luss, Dorothy moaned about "a poor dinner, and sour ale". Yet "as long as people were civil we were contented". Tarbet's hospitality provided "nothing but salt meat and eggs for dinner – no potatoes; the house smelt strongly of herrings, which were hung to dry over the kitchen fire".

Nature, not the works of man, dominated the Highland scene in the Wordsworthian period. What would they have thought of the diesel-trains that clank through the deer-haunted woods near Taynuilt, or the railway bridge strung across the Etive narrows, or the road through Glencoe that now looks like an aircraft runway? Helicopters rise from the outskirts of Oban, some of them on mercy runs to the isles. (The patients are landed on the shinty field within a few yards of the hospital wards.)

I have yet to be disappointed by Highland hospitality. My favourite landlady keeps an immaculate 'hoose' and serves wholesome food, but she runs the place with a cool – if not clinical – efficiency. Enter the house, and she will look at your feet before your face, in case you are bringing in dirt. At 10 p.m., on the dot, she stalks into the lounge and switches off the electric fire, saying: "I like to see the place neat and tidy before *we* all go to bed." One evening I dutifully scampered off to bed. Secure (as I imagined) in my bedroom, I rearranged the hangers in the wardrobe. Several hangers clashed.

Instantly – or so it seemed – the door opened. In stalked the landlady, demanding: "What have *we* broken now?"

1

A Voyage to Inchcailloch

Oh! ye'll tak' the high road and I'll take
    the low road
An' I'll be in Scotland before ye;
But wae is my heart until we meet again
On the bonnie, bonnie banks o' Loch Lomon.

I took a high road to the bonnie banks, crossing the Clyde on the new Erskine Bridge. This cable-stayed, box-girder structure which has a central span of 1,000 feet is high enough to allow for the passage of very big ships on the river. I felt to be dangling from the clouds.

I amused myself by comparing the experiences of the Words-worths with my own impressions of crossing the Clyde. They saw the river for the first time at a point near Lanark, and considered that the banks were poverty-stricken – by which they meant they were not richly endowed with woods and hedges. (The banks I saw were sterilized by concrete, brick and tarmac.)

In 1803, William and Dorothy left Dumbarton at about 11 a.m. under a cheerless sky and in ungenial air, "which we regretted, as we were going to Loch Lomond and wished to greet the first of the Scottish lakes with our cheerfullest and best feelings". (I travelled in conditions well known to photographers as 'cloudy bright' and regained my cheerfulness when I saw the name 'Loch Lomond' painted in large white letters on a road vibrant with heavy lorries.)

Inevitably, the famous song came to mind. A version of the first verse appears above. Who would meet on the bonnie banks of Loch Lomond? The song possibly dates back to the Jacobite period, having echoes of the '45.

Seeing the Kilpatrick Hills, I thought of wolves! It seems that they were common enough here in the fourteenth century for a local tax to be raised to dispose of them. The early tourists were not likely to be savaged by wolves, for a Mr MacQueen had clobbered Scotland's last wolf long before their arrival. Until quite recently, a visitor could feel his or her scalp prickle with excitement near Loch Lomond on seeing bears and Siberian tigers in a special park!

Here and there, the bonnie banks have been tramped flat and hard as concrete by thousands of holidaymakers. It has been estimated that each year some two million people cast their eyes on Loch Lomond. Erskine's hanging bridge makes the journey easier than ever for the English. To Glaswegians, Loch Lomond is a mere twenty or so miles from the city centre. At little more than that distance, a family out for the day can cross the High-land Line, that dislocation of the earth's crust that runs south-westwards from Stonehaven to Helensburgh. Some thirty miles from the city of Glasgow, on impressive hills, red stags roar and ptarmigan – an arctic-type grouse, here at their most southerly station in Britain – keep down their heads as a golden eagle sweeps by. A visitor literally 'dropped in' while I was at Loch Lomond. He arrived by amphibious aircraft, which he left parked on the beach at Rowardennan!

I surveyed Britain's largest expanse of fresh water. Loch Lomond has a length of 25 miles and varies in width from 5 miles at Mid-Ross to 500 yards in the northern stretch. Between Tarbet and Inveruglas, the loch reaches a depth of 653 feet. A man with far more patience than I possess calculated it has a capacity of 93,000 million cubic feet of water – give or take a few hundred gallons!

In blustery weather, the loch is like the sea in captivity. The valley it occupies was scoured by ice in Pleistocene times, and the last of the glaciers melted some 10,000 years ago. Scenically, there are two Loch Lomonds. The northern reach has affinities with a fjord, and it gives way to a broad and relatively shallow southern basin bestrewn with islets. To the north, hills with elevations of over 3,000 feet plunge directly into the loch. The southern area is altogether more gentle in appearance, with some topographical variety brought about by those same geological turmoils which gave us the 'fault' we now call the Highland Line.

It gives a rugged character to a string of islands – Inchcailloch, Torrinch, Creinch, Inchmurrin. Place-names at Loch Lomond indicate by themselves the change of countryside. An island to the south is an 'inch', whereas in the north the name is 'eilean'; this is truly of the Highlands.

Loch Lomond is replenished by Falloch Water, entering to the north, and by Endrick Water (at the south-east), also by many lesser watercourses. Water is drawn off to appease the thirst of people living in Scotland's central belt. Any surplus drains away as a river named Leven. You should also know that the name Lomond is probably derived from Ben Lomond, 'mountain of the beacon', which almost shouts to be noticed as you follow the winding road in the west.

I decided on a novel way of crossing the Highland Line. On previous jaunts I had done this by car, but this time a ferryboat from Balmaha would take me to an uninhabited islet, Inchcailloch, and I would walk across the rocks of the boundary fault. Inchcailloch is one of five islets (plus a small part of the mainland) forming the Loch Lomond Nature Reserve.

At the car park of Balmaha, the last of the season's wasps tried to share a feast of fish and chips (I rejected the idea of buying haggis and chips). Pleasure craft in neat rows fidgeted at their moorings in the bay. I toyed with the idea of crossing to Inchcailloch by leaping from one deck to the next.

Viewed from the mainland shore, well-wooded Inchcailloch looked more like a raft heaped up with vegetation than an island of rock and soil. So insubstantial did it appear, that it could surely be moved by one of the fussy little tugs from the Clyde. Inchcailloch bristles with trees as a hedgehog bristles with spines. Pines bedeck the crest of the ridge. Oaks dominate elsewhere. Some trees extend their branches over the loch.

The name of the island means 'isle of the cowled woman', presumably a nun. Inchcailloch was inhabited long before the monastic period, however, being a part of the old kingdom of the Scoti which extended at its peak of influence to Loch Leven, the Black Mount and Loch Lomond. The Scoti came under the pressure of Norsemen arriving from the west. To the east were the Picts, the 'painted folk'. When the capital of Dunadd (pronounced Doonatt) near Crinan was stormed by the Picts in 844, the Scoti were doubtless demoralized, yet, by what ruse only a specialist in history could relate, a Dalriadan king came to occupy the Pictish throne.

So the Gaelic culture of Ireland spread through most of this wild northern land. It was from Scoti that the very name 'Scotland' sprang, and the name of the old kingdom – Dalriada – is perpetuated by the Dalradian Series, a geological term for the grits, sandstones and shales that are evident near Loch Lomond but also form the Central Highlands.

I did not time the voyage of the ferryboat, but it cannot have exceeded ten minutes. Our departure from Balmaha caused a temporary dispersal of mallard that had been dabbling for food near the jetty. The name 'mallard' should be rendered in inverted commas. As usual, where an absence of human predation encourages wild duck to gather in vast numbers, some had liaised with duck of domestic strains. Hybridization was conspicuous, though a pure mallard drake cruised by the ferryboat and looked a real dandy.

We passed three anglers in a small boat. Were they seeing Britain's most northerly roach, or hoping to hook a pike that was cruising in the shallows? A particularly fine specimen of Loch Lomond pike made the scales dip at 47 pounds.

Loch Lomond's special fish is the powan, a sort of freshwater herring which, being a plankton feeder, is rarely hooked. The only known stocks are in this loch and in Loch Eck. It is believed the fish are descendants of migratory fish which became land-locked at the close of the Ice Age. Wordsworth would have been fascinated by the powan, for his native Cumbria has some species of fish that similarly were land-locked, the best known being the char.

After the voyage, the boat nudged the jetty at North Bay, Inchcailloch, though this slight indentation in the coastline was only just deserving of the title 'bay'. I looked back to see the rocks of the Highland Fault dramatically evident on Conic Hill (1,175 feet); I saw how neatly the hill lined up with the island, which had a spine of the same rock formations.

My feet crunched on shingle as I quested for the start of a nature trail. To have the island to myself for the afternoon was a notable treat, especially as Inchcailloch has had no regular resident for 200 years. Here I was on an unspoilt island – five minutes from civilization.

A muddy slope led me into the gloom of an oak wood occupying the deep soils of the central valley. Well-spaced trees met high above me in a flurry of tinted foliage. A few rents were appearing in the woodland canopy as autumn progressed. Where the sun's rays could reach the ground, plants added splashes of green to the otherwise sombre litter.

As I followed the nature trail, I saw oak give way to the alder of marshy ground and ferns that were a uniform lime-green in the half-light. I gained elevation and, from the side of the main ridge, I scanned the southern basin of the loch, also the deltaic mouth of the River Endrick. As the year wanes, salmon and sea trout enter the Endrick, questing for the gravelly beds where eggs can be deposited. At most times of the year, the loch itself is broken by the dark forms of cormorants. To the Endrick marshes in autumn come a variety of birds. Up to eighty whooper swans guzzle the waterweed, and over 1,000 grey geese have been counted here. Most of the geese are greylags, but whitefronts form a small but increasing winter population here.

Autumn days by Endrick are full of promise. A hen harrier beats the bounds. Short-eared owls fly by day, looking like soft brown moths. An osprey sometimes lingers here to fish on southern migration. Loch Lomond – more precisely Inch Galbraith – was a nesting place of ospreys, but the last pair to be seen here flew in 1869. Shooting ospreys with the greatly improved guns gave pleasure to a few Highland sportsmen. John Colquhoun was the villain who despatched the last local birds.

I could not pretend that I was the first visitor to Inchcailloch since antiquity. Before long my boots rang with a hollow sound on wooden steps and raised boards provided by the Nature Conservancy Council, and at the summit stood a wooden seat! I recall that a patch of bell heather flowered near one of its legs. Behind the seat were large pines; before it a broom, covered with dark pods, hinting at the advancing season.

Looking out from the summit of Inchcailloch, I saw the world degenerate into grey washes. Now even the mighty Ben Lomond was just a blodge of dark grey against greys of slightly lighter hues. I felt to be viewing a gigantic water-colour painting, impetuously executed of washes applied by a large brush. Until that moment I had not realized how many greys were possible. At one end of the tonal range, the greys verged on pink; at the other end on mauve.

I was mentally unprepared for the profusion and variety of islands. There appeared to be hundreds, but in fact the loch holds only thirty of reasonable size. The names fall from the tongue of a native like droplets from a waterfall – Inchmurrin, Clairinch, Torrinch . . .

The first-mentioned is also the largest, some two miles in length. Inchfad, just ahead, was mainly grassland, merely edged with trees. Some of these islands have permanent homes upon them, and the ferryman from Balmaha is also the postman. Whenever there is a general election, you can rely on a television company shooting off film of the island folk, wearing tartan, being brought to the mainland in order to record their votes.

Fontane, a visitor in the nineteenth century, described Loch Lomond as The Lake with Many Islands, which he compared with great water-lilies. He also noticed that the mountains to the north do not appear to crowd the loch because everything is on the grand scale. He thought the hills were "more like satellites . . . for the position of these lovely mountains, which sometimes attain a height of three thousand feet, is such that one always remains in the centre of their circular dance and has always got them around one – like the moon when on a clear night you drive for miles through the fields".

A French visitor, B. Faujas St. Fond, remembered minor features – the fine sunlight, silvery rocks, flowery and verdant mosses, black oxen, white sheep, shepherds beneath the pines.

I would strongly advise any shepherd to avoid resting by pine trees when a gale is blowing. On the summit of Inchcailloch is the terrible evidence of a wind's ferocity – pines with limbs shattered, pines tumbled (to be left where they fell as a home for insects and fungi) and pines with their top knots severely thinned. A terrifying month was January 1968. The gale then ravaging the district also flattened trees on two and a half miles of land in the Queen Elizabeth Forest to the east.

The woodland through which I descended to Port Bawn was strangely silent. I had hoped to flush the capercaillie, largest grouse in the world. This species became extinct in Britain but was reintroduced, from Scandinavian stock, by Breadalbane of

Taymouth. The first bird I heard call on Inchcailloch was a wren, which offered a torrent of rapid, terse notes. It stood, tail acock, on a tangle of vegetation that had sprung from the base of a tree.

A guelder rose enlivened the wood as does an orchid in the tropical jungle. It was while looking at the flowers that I heard a rasping sound. I had the quiet confidence that I was listening to the noise made by the claws of a squirrel as it climbed a nearby tree. The squirrel could not resist sneaking another view of me. I saw the blunt head of a grey squirrel, not that of the red variety with which I have had many delightful encounters in Highland woods. The grey comes from North America. Having spread rapidly across England (where it is the darling of many suburban housewives), it must now be poised to invade the Highlands. But will it fare as well as the red squirrel in the big Highland conifer forests, to the life of which the red has had thousands of years to adapt?

Another rasping sound indicated that the squirrel was moving again and was now high above the ground. I may have surprised it as it fed in the litter. Autumn is a bountiful time, producing on Inchcailloch an abundance of acorns.

The boatman had told me of the 'white deer' – the fallow. It is claimed that those roaming by Loch Lomond are descendants of stock brought to the district in the early part of the fourteenth century by Robert the Bruce, who used Inchcailloch as a hunting preserve. No fallow showed their faces while I was on the island, but there were signs of their presence in the way a holly had been browsed, bark on young trees was damaged, and mud by the path impressed by the slots of moderately large deer.

A young roebuck gazed at me from forty yards; we stared intently at each other for perhaps two minutes before mild interest and curiosity in the deer led to excitement, followed by the inevitable headlong flight. I tried unsuccessfully to arrest the roebuck's attention by giving a few gruff barks.

The roebuck, an accomplished swimmer, could easily reach an island in Loch Lomond. Once, while scanning a Highland loch for a view of waterfowl, I saw what appeared to be a periscope. It was a side view of the head of roebuck that was swimming vigorously.

Port Bawn: the name suggests a hive of activity, but there was no one to be seen. Waves had heaped sand in the little bay. I returned to the path and crossed the hard rocks of the Highland boundary fault.

Chest-high bracken blotted out the site of an old farmstead, which was used until, in about 1770, timber-growing was introduced and oaks were planted on the pastures and meadows. For about 130 years, Inchcailloch periodically heard the thwack of woodman's axe against coppice wood. The aim was to supply oak bark for tanning and timber for a distillery at Balmaha where vinegar, wood tar and dyeing stuffs were produced.

I stood, alone, in the old burial ground, musing on death! Not even a wren called. Tall trees hemmed in a plot holding the foundations of a Christian church which have been dated to the thirteenth century. An old story relates that St Kentigern(a), an early Christian missionary, was laid to rest on Inchcailloch. I already knew of his reputation from my travels in Cumbria, and presumably the Wordsworths had heard of him. He raised a cross near where Keswick stands – the place is still known as Crosthwaite – and by his nickname, Mungo, he is remembered in Mungrisedale near the Skiddaw range, an area of large pastures, sheep, and lean men who scarcely ever move without collie dogs.

A hoary tradition asserts that island burials were popular because here the bodies could not be tampered with by wolves. I prefer to think of the popularity of island interments in a religious sense – as symbolic of the passing over Jordan to the Hereafter.

There was, in the burial ground, a terrible silence, which is a prime prerequisite for contemplation. I noticed three headstones, on which were carved in relief a sheep, cow and farming implements. Casually walking over to the grave adorned by a sheep, I looked at it. It bore my own name – William Mitchell!

Looking back on Inchcailloch from the boat, I saw its dome of leaves that, having soaked up the summer sunshine, was now crinkled, tinted, ready to be cast. Inchcailloch was a peaceful island. I could recall only the song of the wren, the rasp of a squirrel's claws on wood and, down by the jetty, the thin autumn ditty of a robin.

2

Big Ben

An irrepressible Cockney I met while climbing Ben Lomond called the hill Big Ben. Perhaps by using this name he felt at home on this most southerly of Scotland's 3,000-foot peaks. To most people, it is The Ben – a friendly giant that is part of the Highlands, but "nobbut just" as they say in northern England.

See Ben Lomond from west of the loch, and it is high browed, with padded shoulders. When seen from the east – as from Aberfoyle – it vies with Schiehallion, having the shape of a cone. The distinctive outline was chosen as the motif for the Queen Elizabeth Forest Park.

During the climb to the summit of Ben Lomond, I managed rather more than one mile an hour, an achievement that was nowhere near good enough to feature in a Scottish book of records. I dawdled, in fact, being interested in natural life as it exists at different elevations. I was never in danger of losing the track, which had been beaten to concrete hardness by thousands of boots.

Down by the loch, at Rowardennan, lay car parks and litter bins and an outstanding new toilet block made of timber. Here, too, was the amphibious aircraft to which I have already referred. It stood on the shingle, a few yards from lapping water, like some bizarre monster that had hauled itself out of the loch to bask in the thin sunlight.

I plodded through an area of conifers – quite young trees, something less than twenty years old. My boots were given sound-proofing by a tawny mat of spent conifer needles. I remember the stillness in which a sudden outburst from a blue tit had something of the vibrancy of a pneumatic drill.

Trees were left behind at about 1,000 feet, and now I strode by bracken, then heather, then blaeberry. Near the Halfway Well, a track went off eastwards towards the heart of the Forest

Park. A raven barked; two birds were gliding high. One of them playfully turned on its back. Wing-flapping is wasteful of energy! The raven is a master of harnessing the power of uprushing air. I have seen birds simply step into space and be carried aloft by the wind. A bird that peered at me as I stood near its nest seemed to be hanging from the sky, and had simply lowered its legs to help it maintain its balance in a blustery north-easter.

At the summit of Ben Lomond, I moved across grassland to the craggy areas. I was looking for ptarmigan, the arctic grouse which must have been generally distributed in Scotland in the wake of the Ice Ages but now remain faithful to a few hilltops, the nearest approximation to the tundra. A few ptarmigan are found on the peaks arrayed at the head of Loch Lomond, including The Ben.

Ptarmigan cling to their gale-blasted hilltops and by moulting three times a year they keep in harmony with tonal variations as the seasons come and go. Autumn is a benevolent time, offering various berries as food. In winter, the bird keeps its life ticking over by feeding on the tips of heather plants – and often little else.

Most birds quit the high ground in winter, but the ptarmigan is not often seen below 2,000 feet. There is a local eminence called Ptarmigan whose crest is at 2,398 feet. And lying under the hill, not far from the loch, is Ptarmigan Lodge. It amazes me that the ptarmigan can survive on the small 'island' that is the summit of Ben Lomond. Disturbance is regular. Someone may be found on the hill on every day of the year.

I saw one of the grey-lichened rocks move. Or so I thought. A ptarmigan walked, and then ran, seemingly anxious to avoid flight. The bird, grey-backed, with white beneath and part-way up its sides, looked half as old as the rocks against which it had crouched. When it first moved, it really did seem that a piece of landscape had been infused with life. As the bird took to the air, I saw its white wings flashing.

One ptarmigan and two ravens were the only birds I saw on Ben Lomond that day. The red deer living north of the hill were at their siesta, but come dusk and the hinds would move out to feed under the supervision of masterful stags. The red stag menaces many an autumn day with its roaring, and sometimes a visitor will hear a dry rattle, as though two men were sparring with walking sticks. A rival pair have temporarily locked their antlers and are engaged in a pushing match.

Listen, too, for a sharp crack – the sound made when the heads of two rival billy goats have collided. Autumn is mating time in the world of the wild goat, and a small group of goats exists near Ben Lomond. Amorous males charge at each other, and if any creature knows the miseries of headache it is surely a billy after such an encounter! A cloying, distasteful smell hangs about a male goat. The tang is distasteful to humans, but presumably sends a female into raptures. A friend has a theory that a billy goat always moves into the wind so that it does not smell itself!

Goats were tethered at many Highland farms and villages in the days before the Clearances. So valuable were the animals that a tenant might pay rent in goat kids, and when a human mother's milk failed a bairn would be reared on the ultra-rich milk from the goat herd. The nourishment in goat milk was locked up in cheese to be eaten in the winter. When the black-faced sheep took over the hills, and glens were depopulated, many goats simply reverted to the wild state. Shepherds were pleased to see them in craggy areas, where they cropped the first flush of grass from ledges – grass that might have tempted a sheep, with fatal consequences. What matter if yet another goat fell to its death?

Gone from the flanks of Ben Lomond are the legions of mountain or blue hares remembered by the old folk. Like the ptarmigan, this hilltop hare has a number of coats, donned in bewildering succession to match the seasonal variations. The coat is white in winter – but the tips of the blunt-tipped ears remain black. To be sure of seeing the mountain hare today, one should visit the blocky hills of Perthshire. One Easter evening, on a moorland road near Loch Tay, I counted 350 hares before I succumbed to boredom and, instead, settled down to watch the beasties. Because the moorland was devoid of snow, the hares stood out with great clarity.

What did the Wordsworths think of Ben Lomond? They viewed it first from west of the loch – and were not impressed; it lacked massiveness and simplicity, "perhaps from the top being broken into three distinctive stages". Perhaps, indeed, the rain had lowered their morale.

I remember Ben Lomond for its crowning glory – the dark cragland around the corries to the north and east of the true summit. I had little else to see. Mist had draped itself across every horizon, and the majestic bens around the head of Loch Lomond – also the twin-peaked Ben Venue, above Loch Katrine – were indistinct. Loch Lomond itself, far below, gleamed faintly in the murk.

The Cockney who called the hill Big Ben told me he was walking along the West Highland Way – 92 miles to Fort William – and he had allowed five days for this excursion. Now retired from work, he lived a solitary life as a bachelor, without close living relatives, and had nothing better to do than walk! I watched him go off at the sort of brisk pace a man develops if he has daily caught the 8.15 train to the city throughout a long working life.

My excursion to the crag-faces of Ben Lomond had begun early with a drive through the Pass of Balmaha to the westernmost area of the Forest Park. Today we see forestry on a grand scale, extending over many square miles. Much of it has the bluey look imparted by sitka spruce, now the most popular commercial timber of the west.

The Lomondside of old grew majestic oaks. Stout timber of this kind was in demand by local shipbuilders as early as 1494. When it was decided to make a "great row barge" at that time, a party of joiners and carpenters was sent to a wooded islet on Loch Lomond to fell the necessary timber. A few centuries later, thousands of woodmen whose names are now forgotten sustained quite a number of local woodland industries. Among them were charcoal burners, the charcoal being needed for iron-smelting.

I walked through a modern plantation. The trees were spaced at regular intervals. In the air was a strong resinous tang. Charcoal burners working in the old deciduous woods lived roughly during the time a pitstead was smoking. This neat heap of wood, covered with soil, must smoulder and not be allowed to burst into flames. The faces of the men had the appearance of mahogany from their skilful and smoky job.

Picturing them at work was not difficult. A few weeks before my Scottish jaunt I met a Cumbrian, Jack Allonby, whose mind was a repository of the lore of charcoal burning; he remembered it vividly from his youth. I saw him construct for a history-inclined friend the type of living hut he saw being used by members of his own family and friends who had to work in distant woods.

Jack Allonby was born, reared and worked in the woods of Furness, at the southern edge of Cumbria. The routine carried out here would be similar to that practised in parts of western Scotland, for when the Furness woods were denuded, iron ore was shipped from Furness to those parts of Scotland still abounding in timber. For example, some of these ships tied up at a pier in Loch Etive.

The Wordsworths, good Cumbrians, were rowed to some of the islands in Loch Lomond in 1803 and saw huts made by woodmen. Each hut was shaped like a boat. The men slept on logs bestrewn with straw. A forked branch that dangled from the roof held their kettle over an open fire.

Jack Allonby remembers small shelters being made by the charcoal burners near the pitsteads. The living hut was a more commodious structure. It consisted of a low circular wall made without a dab of mortar and breached in two places, for hearth and doorway. The superstructure was timbering covered with sods, and so it resembled a raised wigwam. The hut was adequate for four or five men living here for several days at a time, and building such a structure could be done quickly; all the materials for its construction and subsequent repair were to hand.

The circular wall kept out larger animals and added considerably to the height within. The fire warmed the men and also kept fungi at bay. Rushes were spread on the floor, and to make a bed a man would drive four pronged sticks into the ground, stretching poles between them and covering the intervening spaces with birch branches. A man slept in his clothes.

Sauntering through part of the forest, I found a twiggy platform some twenty feet up a conifer; a nest built on a cluster of branches. It had been made by a pair of sparrow-hawks, woodland fiends the very mention of which makes the face of a gamekeeper florid. The sparrow-hawk is now protected by law.

The previous day I watched a sparrow-hawk sailing high overhead as it moved to another hunting ground. From a distance it bore a close resemblance to the cuckoo, being greyish with a long tail giving the impression that the wings were set far forward. Later, a sparrow-hawk kept me company as I motored along a straight stretch of road. The bird was patrolling a hedge, gliding with occasional flaps of its rounded wings. The long tail gave this bird a fine degree of manoeuvrability.

In autumn, the young hawks are dispersing; the nests in which they were reared are forsaken, and it is rare for a pair of sparrow-hawks to turn to a specific nest a second time. In some northerly districts, you may find sparrow-hawks nesting on birch trees. Nests in hardwood areas are not rare. However, the coniferous forest is the preferred habitat, and so extensive are the new plantings that sparrow-hawks will thrive as never before.

In a young forest, larch rather than spruce is the chosen tree. In a larch wood, the birds have space to go to and from their nest, and the tree puts out rigid branches at appropriate heights. There is sufficient canopy to keep out the worst of the weather. Trees in a spruce plantation tend to jostle closely together, restricting the movement of birds.

Seeing the sparrow-hawks near Loch Lomond reminded me of many days spent watching the woodland fiends. I recalled the display flights at first light, the tittering call of a female as she left the nest to receive food from the male, the fierce, unblinking stares of young birds cocooned in white down. Sparrow-hawks nest in a quiet world. In a larch plantation the sounds of a busy world are muted; you can actually hear your clothes rustling!

Sparrow-hawks delay their nesting until such a time that the young are crying out for food when it is abundant. The world is half-full of inexperienced young birds that are easily flown-down and killed by the male. Ultimately, the young of sparrow-hawk are being offered birds as large as pheasant poults. Some nests I have seen have dripped with blood!

The female stays at or near the nest. The hunter male brings food to a 'plucking stool' – a hummock at the edge of the plantation or in cases known to me some fallen tree beside a forest road. The 'plucking stool' becomes littered with feathers of the prey.

A nest that is being used is bestrewn with fine down and a few feathers from the female; she goes through a moult while in-cubating. The first egg is laid usually about 12 May and reclines in a shallow depression on the big twiggy nest. Disturb a sparrow-hawk at this time, and she goes off the nest with a clattering sound from her wings; it is similar to the noise made by a flushed wood-pigeon. During the period of incubation, she sits hard. Standing near the nesting tree, I have looked up to see her long tail extending beyond the rim of the nest.

When this hawk was moving, local blackbirds would give clattering cries that continued for some time after the bird had passed. Local bird life was untroubled by the hawks, which preferred to collect food from areas up to two miles away, and the evening song of thrushes included the tittering call of the female sparrow-hawk. Indeed, the thrushes told me much about hawks. I got into the way of listening to them to confirm the presence of a local pair. A blackbird is less imaginative. Its song is stereotyped, a repetition of a few simple phrases.

One evening in mid-May the remains of a woodcock were found at the 'plucking stool'. Shortly afterwards I saw a wood-cock roding – beating the bounds of its territory, flying some fifty feet above the ground, and periodically uttering three grunts and a squeak. Two birds, clashing at the edge of their territories, called excitedly, but soon broke off the encounter and flew their separate ways.

The young from this nest flew in early July, pitching down awkwardly on trees round about. They were playful sessions – aerial games in which adults and young were lively – and with the coming of autumn the family broke up.

Old-time writers give us an idea of the richness of wildlife before the Sporting Age, when so many birds and beasts were threatened in the interests of game. Pennant, visiting the Loch Lomond district in 1777, reported that roe deer were quite common, and this is their status today. Writing only twenty-two years after Pennant's visit, a local pastor named Stuart listed the pine marten and polecat among the quadrupeds. They are no longer present.

The jay is much more common than it was, but in the Scottish context is still curiously local in its range. Pre-eminently a bird of hardwood areas, it benefits from a local profusion of oaks and in autumn gorges itself on acorns. Some acorns are stored away for future use. Many a fine oak was planted by a jay!

The jay's villainous character is accentuated by its black

moustachial stripes. During the nesting season it rifles the nests of many woodland birds. A friend saw a jay kill a blue tit in cold blood. The tit, having picked up a morsel at a bird table, flew with it to a large tree. A jay, alighting beside the tit, suddenly grabbed the bird in its beak, banged it against the branch and dropped its lifeless body to the ground.

Jays that I saw in flight were conspicuous because of their white rump patches. It was not necessary to see a jay to know it was present. Staying near an oakwood, I was awakened at dawn by the harsh screeching of the local birds.

I motored around the southern end of Loch Lomond, and then headed northwards for Luss and Tarbet. The Wordsworths were told that the Highlands began at Luss. At the time of their visit, great changes were coming to the district. Old-style houses, roughly fashioned, with thatch on the roof and a hole to let out the smoke from the fire – they were, noted a visitor, "like smoking dunghills" – were giving way to substantial stone buildings.

Crossing a neck of low land between Tarbet (Loch Lomond) and Arrochar (Loch Long), I thought of the brilliant tactics of a Norse leader who, in 1263, sailed his longboats up Loch Long and had them hauled across to Loch Lomond, where they descended on unsuspecting communities. To Robert Burns, Arrochar was "a land of savage hills, swept by savage rains, peopled by savage sheep, tended by savage people". Had the local food disagreed with him? Ben Arthur blocks out half the sky and terminates with a group of rocks called The Cobbler. Dorothy Wordsworth saw them in mist, when "the strange figures appeared and disappeared, like living things".

Reading Dorothy's journal, I sensed her excitement when Loch Long came into sight. For this is a sea loch. Everything about the sea has novelty for a person living many miles from the coast. She mentioned "the waves breaking among stones overgrown with yellow weed; the fishermen's boats and other larger vessels . . . lying at anchor near the opposite shore; sea-birds flying overhead; the noise of torrents mingling with the beating of the waves". The valley, enclosed by misty mountains, was "a melancholy but not a dreary scene".

On the day of my visit, dreariness had set in with rain. The district was overhung by dense cloud. Herring gulls wailed as though weary of the weather, and the powder-blue plumage of herons was only a little darker than the mist. Wading birds from the northlands crossed the tidelines in such dense groups they were like puffs of smoke.

The tide was 'lazy', unflurried by wind, and so quiet that I clearly heard the sound of water tumbling off the hills.

Someone, someday, will interview those people – now middle-aged to elderly – who were tourists in the 'good old days' when roads were poor, in many cases unsurfaced, resembling dried-up river beds. Such people will have some stirring tales to tell of exploring the Highlands the hard way.

Travel is now an easy matter. I stopped near Loch Long to see a new road extending as a broad sweep towards the Rest and Be Thankful. That name had a grim significance in the eighteenth century. It was first used by the soldiers who built the old road.

I stopped on the way to the summit to admire the hard masculinity of Ben Arthur's foothills, and also to peer into Glencroe which, deep, smooth-sided, was like a fingermark pressed deeply into the landscape. The Brack and also Ben Donich wore skirts of green, composed of conifers. The trees neither broke the skylines nor poached on the floor of the glen. Scale was indicated by a small building with while walls and red roof; it looked like a child's toy.

Relict lengths of the old road now toned well with the landscape; they were fast becoming part of it as they crumbled. Over the summit, I saw a sparkle on Loch Restil and another smooth stretch of road leading down to Loch Fyne. A roadside sign proclaimed: "White Heather Roots for Sale".

It was a delight to see bare hills, men, collies and sheep. A gathering of sheep was in hand, and the animals spilled down a brackeny hillside. The steady pace of the men in this steep terrain impressed. A hill shepherd once told me: "When this pace goes, laddie, I goes!"

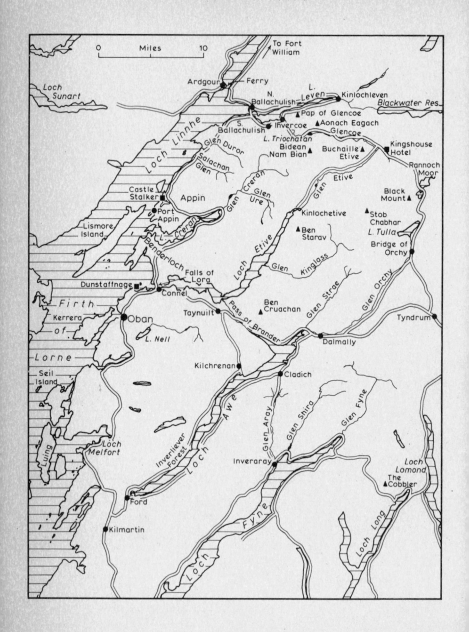

3

Fair Glen Shira

Loch Fyne is an arm of the sea, but it lacked the oceanic bluster. The tide seemed to have wearied itself on its long run from open water. With no wind to stir it up, salt water simply smacked its lips on a shore strewn with yellow weed. So calm was the water that circling gulls could admire their reflections.

A hooded crow – the bird Lea MacNally has called "the evil spirit of the hills" – looked quite docile as it spent the day beach-combing. It would carry a shellfish aloft, drop it in the hope it would be shattered by hitting a rock, and then pick among the broken pieces for the fleshy contents.

Grey feathers on mantle and underparts marked out this 'whoodie' from the all-black carrion crows of more southerly districts. A local boy had wrapped his tongue round the bird's name and rendered it 'whoodie'.

It was an afternoon so still and warm that a few butterflies had been tempted into action. A red admiral sunbathed on a patch of waste ground within three yards of the open beach. Red admirals sometimes appear in the hill country as summer gives way to autumn, and they can be seen resting on flowering plants by the burns.

I scanned the hills around Loch Fyne. Some of them held colonies of Britain's only true alpine butterfly, the mountain ringlet, which here has been recorded as low down as 1,500 feet. This far-from-showy creature is brownish, banded with dull orange on the fore and hind wings. For thousands of years, in late summer, it has enlivened the high, moist grassland of Argyll with its flighting.

An associated butterfly, the Scotch argus, is another grass-feeder, preferring a lightly-wooded area. In August, I saw hundreds of these handsome, dark butterflies moving over the stems of grasses. With a setting of wizened vegetation, the

LONDON BOROUGH OF REDBRIDGE 77/42003

butterflies looked black.

One alighted on my arm. I saw the wings were dark but velvety brown, with lighter bands and spots that resembled eyes. The larva, tinged with brown, matches in tone the grasses on which it feeds.

It was tempting to drive straight into Inveraray, whose white buildings were complemented by dazzling water and a sky bedecked by cumulus cloud. Instead, I turned to enter Glen Shira for a spirited walk. The road is private; eventually a gate prevents the unauthorized motorist from going further, but I have found that a pedestrian who keeps to the road is tolerated.

So I trudged, beside lime and sweet chestnut, into a valley visited by the notable guests of the Argylls during the nineteenth century. They travelled in horse-drawn carriages. Queen Victoria and Prince Albert were here in 1847. Harriet Beecher Stowe, the author of *Uncle Tom's Cabin,* was shown Rob Roy's cottage (of which, today, only part of a wall remains).

All admired the Dubh Loch (*dubh* means black). When I reached this shallow stretch of water, which receives the River Shira and overflows as the River Garron, I was in time to see a little grebe floating, high in the water like a cork. The buoyant appearance was further emphasized by an upturned bill and jaunty rump. The rump had a sawn-off appearance!

A red-breasted merganser paddled furiously away, and then took cover from a shoreline bedecked with reed. Much bolder were the swans – a family group, the young still wearing a dull brown plumage. The water of this 'black loch' was so clear, indeed, I saw the webbed feet of the birds working like huge paddles, and I contrasted a tranquil scene with memories of a day on a sea loch, with the water grey and choppy and mute swans lumbering into the air like overburdened flying boats. The birds may be vocally mute, but their wings produce a humming sound, like haunting music.

An avenue of great beeches used to lead to the Dubh Loch. I remember the alders that stood darkly against the bright water of the River Shira. One tree had half its exposed roots in water. (Alders growing on a pebbly beach by Loch Lomond appeared to be standing on tiptoe. Light was visible between the trelliswork of their roots. When the loch is full, these alders are surrounded by water.)

Even in early autumn, local hillsides were still as blue as a summer sky, the effect of flowering scabious. The road was verged by tall grasses where red admiral butterflies flaunted their bright wings. I saw a meadow brown; a male, its forewings patched by orange. A peacock butterfly alighted on a thistle. I climbed steadily, blinkered by trees which forced me to concentrate on such sights near at hand.

Then the glen rang with a bird call, *wheeoo, wheeoo*. Finding a gap in the aisle of conifers, I looked across the valley to where a pair of buzzards glided lazily on their broad wings. A buzzard, breaking the skyline, showed its underparts, with the distinctive dark forewing.

The road I followed was a considerable improvement on that seen during a previous visit. A new road was needed when the upper glen was dammed for hydro-electricity and when the Forestry Commission began to deck the hills with spruce.

Explosives had been used by the road-makers. Cliffs with raw edges came into view, and already plant life was colonizing the rock faces. Mosses were encouraged to grow by flowing water that was so shallow the rock appeared to be pulsing. I saw clumps of fading yellow mountain saxifrage. The road verge and bases of the cliffs were speckled by the white blossoms of Grass of Parnassus. Each stem, rising above a rosette of heart-shaped leaves, supported a single white flower, though to describe a flower simply as white would fail to do it justice. Each petal was delicately veined with green. And from each tuft of flowers came a fine honey tang.

When I rested my elbows on a bridge built across a ravine, a cascade of chacking fieldfares flew from rowans that had rooted in rock crevices, far down, out of my sight.

I returned to the Dubh Loch. The swans had moved to the far bank. The little grebe dived with a plop. When I next saw Loch Fyne, the tide was running out and Inveraray appeared to be on a ridge lying above a wet beach. The Wordsworths, reaching this town when the tide was in, felt to be on the edge of a large, almost circular lake.

At Inveraray the buildings are in harmony. Almost all of them were constructed in the second half of the eighteenth century. In a wave of inspiration and enthusiasm, the old town was swept away and a new town built, and thus Argyll acquired an attractive county town and the Duke of Argyll a new castle.

The old Inveraray had nothing to impress visitors; they tended instead to dwell on the climate and situation. Mrs Elizabeth Montagu, writing to a friend in 1759, mentioned the cold climate and rude inhabitants, a soil uncultivated, and "all the accomplishments of savage greatness". She now understood why the Duke of Argyll spent much of the year in England! When Dr Johnson (1773) heard of the Duke's plans, he admired the total defiance of all expense. The Duke died as his grand plans were being put into effect, but in 1785 the traveller John Knox saw that local people were well lodged in houses of stone, lime and slate.

Before long, the weather was again a major point of comment by visitors. The Hon. Mrs Sarah Murray, of Kensington, thought that Inveraray was the noblest place in Scotland, but the climate was dreadful. She asked a lady if the streets were ever dry. The lady said: "Never!"

Nathaniel Wraxall, who came to this district in 1813, looked critically at the new castle, and then considered that if it stood in Middlesex it would be considered barbarous and hideous, "but here on the Banks of a Loch in the Highlands, to which there is hardly any access from more civilised Portions of Scotland, this Castle, rising up in the Desert, impresses with admiration".

I toured the main rooms of Inveraray Castle a few months before they were swept by fire. Here was evidence of life on the grand scale. Then, five miles down the road from Inveraray, I spent an hour or two pottering around the old farming township of Auchindrain which, run by a trust, is being conserved as a museum of Highland farming life.

The castle stood aloof, screened by trees. The old buildings of Auchindrain, some thatched, others with 'tin' roofs of scarlet hue, were visible from the road. Castle and township were closely connected, for the folk of Auchindrain were tenants of the Duke, paying a communal rent. They annually drew lots for the strips of land that were to be cultivated.

At the castle, the Dukes of Argyll had privacy. A resident of Auchindrain could not sneeze without the fact instantly becoming known to all the others. At one time the township was home to over seventy people. It was a self-contained community – the sort that will return when the world's stock of oil runs out and a rising population begins to outstrip the major food supplies.

The Auchindrain experience was vivid. I could easily picture the dark nights of years ago when people assembled round fires of peat turves to yarn or do craft work. The peat-fire flame would remind them of the hard work of cutting turves, rearing them up to dry in sunshine and breeze, and moving them to the buildings. Each household would need about 15,000 turves a year. The candles used at that time were made from mutton grease.

This was a community dedicated to hard work. An imaginative visitor would hear the clack and shutter of the handloom, the ring of hammer against anvil at the smithy, and swish of milk against buckets as cows were milked by hand. Milk was converted into butter and cheese. Potatoes were grown using dung and seaweed as fertilizers. Mutton, salted down in autumn, was consumed in winter. The local people fished for herring in Loch Fyne.

Back at Inveraray, I enjoyed non-stop variety without charge: the entertainment provided by anglers operating from the pier-head. They were fishing for pleasure. In the eighteenth century, fishing was a serious, vital occupation. The whole town stank of herring, and so important was this fish to the local economy that it was featured on the civic coat of arms.

Do not expect to catch a herring on a rod and line. The shoals of fish in Loch Fyne live in the deep channel and dine on plankton. They are caught by means of nets. Loch Fyne kippers have a national renown. When local herrings have been cured and then smoked over oak, the flesh remains quite pale, and the kipper is so pliable that if you drew it over the edge of your hand it would follow the contours. Some kippers commercially produced today are dark brown, like pieces of mahogany, and so stiff you could sole your boots with them.

The herring fleet of old Inveraray consisted of hundreds of boats manned by about 2,000 men. The fishing season extended from July through to January. The men became obsessed with fishing – as indeed they must in those pre-welfare days – and worked from dawn to dusk six days a week. Pennant was told that "on the Sabbath, each boat approaches the land and psalmody and devotion divide the day". Fish salted in barrels sustained a profitable export trade.

The fishery declined because the herring seemed to bypass Loch Fyne. Tourism helped to restore local prosperity. The overland journey was daunting, but in summer a steamboat left Glasgow on a Saturday and voyaged 100 miles to Inveraray, remained off the town on Sunday and returned to Glasgow on Monday. When the steamship arrived at Inveraray, beds and even meals were at a premium.

Herring have not forsaken Loch Fyne, but if there is a tremor of excitement today it is when the salmon are running. These lordly fish are still netted under ancient right. The water appears to boil when there is a good sea trout run.

Another 'lazy' tide established itself in Loch Fyne. From the pierhead at Inveraray I saw a flotilla of eider being tideborne to the mussel beds. Herons brought to this misty Scottish loch something of the character of an old Japanese print, and jellyfish in full sail went grandly by . . .

4

A Whistle in the Night

Evening, somewhere in Kintyre. With spine-chilling abruptness, a whistle cuts the air in a darkening wood. The outburst begins at a fairly low pitch, climbing and then descending in a lovely crescent of sound. Moments later comes a second whistle, similar in duration and quality to the first. Then a third whistle is heard. This is not so well developed and it ends flatly, as though the whistler has run short of breath.

The calling of a sika stag during the early part of the rut is surely the strangest of the animal noises to be heard in Scotland. At mating time, a red stag roars, and the sound can be bovine in character, prompting one visitor to say on his return to a Highland guest house: "Some old cows are bawling up the glen"! A fallow buck can be heard grunting, and the voice of the roebuck is a bark.

Who would expect a medium-sized deer like the sika to whistle? This animal is about the size of a fallow, and therefore quite substantial. The stag I heard in Kintyre was proclaiming his presence to the hinds by blowing down his nose. The alarm whistle of a sika is frequently like the whistle of a bird.

The sikine rut brought excitement to wooded parts of the peninsula in which can be found Scotland's largest concentration of sika deer. These are newcomers to the North. The whistling deer evolved in Asia, across a crescent of land edging up to the Pacific, and on some of the offshore islands. The Japanese type, which is the smallest, is most commonly seen in Britain. About 120 years ago a stock of sika was brought to an estate in Ireland, thence to England and in stages to parts of Scotland. Sika are now up in Sutherland, where some of them are denizens of almost impenetrable spruce forest.

A sika stag begins the rut with new antlers that are branched in a simple way. Gone is the hairy skin called velvet which protected the soft tissue in a growing season that began in April. The new headgear is hard and the stag burnishes it as it rubs against trees and threshes the vegetation. Dirt and resin, lodging in the guttering of the antlers, adds character to their appearance. The best-looking antlers are the dirtiest!

Gone from the stag is the gleaming summer coat of dappled chestnut. Now he wears a thick winter coat and a mane gives him a thick-necked appearance. The general colour is grey-brown, but it can look chocolate-brown in dull light. A faint dappling is seen towards the rump and is an echo of the summer pelage.

The general drabness is relieved by white hairs. They are thickest and longest at the rump, where in recline they stand out with the clarity of a white dinner plate. When the animal is curious or excited, this caudal disc flares out, assuming a heart-shape. White hairs cling to the underpart of the body, and also to the tops of the inner legs, while the white hair at the hock glands is now at its most prominent because the legs are dark.

The sika deer of Kintyre were not easy to follow by a stranger like myself. I had one fairly good view of a stag and hinds, and heard some assorted rustlings in thick cover, an indication that some deer were departing. I was at a disadvantage, not having a deep knowledge of the ground. When I was in the open, I could not see deer in the gloom of a wood, but they could clearly watch my every movement. Peter Delap has likened this situation to that of a dear old lady looking at the world from behind lace curtains and knowing that the world cannot see her in return.

I did find evidence of a stag with the rutting fever upon him. Stumbling across a wallowing place, I felt the excitement that Robinson Crusoe must have known when he beheld the footprint made by Man Friday. My 'Friday footprint' was a saucer-like depression, recently used, for it had not yet filled with water trickling from the land round about. The smooth mud in the wallow held imprints of sikine hair; impressions that were as sharp and fine as lines on a Victorian etching.

Mud that was still drying out lay round about and some of it was plastered on vegetation. I pictured the stag as, lumbering from his mudbath, he threshed the grasses round about. Main paths in the area were cut about by the sharp-edged cleaves of a stag.

As the year declines grandly, with a flurry of autumn-tinted leaves, with frost and pockets of mist, the sika deer goes into raptures as the mating urge overtakes him. For months on end a stag has divided his day between grazing and resting. Parties of stags live apart from the hinds, but in autumn they move back into the areas occupied by the females. A stag claims an area and the hinds that go with it.

Meanwhile, the resident stag lays down scent, a deterrent to other stags. Wallowing is one way of doing this. Another is the rubbing of the head – and its glands – against the ground and vegetation. The wallow I found had a rank smell about it, but my nose could not detect the finer scents which must surely be present in the world of an animal so well endowed with scent glands.

I sometimes yearn for what might be called a smellometer – a device to heighten the perception of the human nose! Trails of scent are left across the countryside by wild mammals. A stretch of woodland reeks with scents unknown in Araby. I have seen young sika stags, hitherto tolerated by the masters but now discouraged, excitedly following the scent trails left by a stag and his retinue of hinds.

On this last occasion I watched a sika stag wallowing – it was at what has been picturesquely called "the edge o' dark". I had overlooked the deer because it was but a dark mass against dark mud. Then I saw a thistle moving. The thistle was horizontal, a few feet from the ground! The stag had peevishly threshed the plant, which had broken off to become lodged between the trez tines.

This stag had flopped in the wallow and was not rolling over. I saw him rise, his chest and underparts and legs being dark and dripping. He rubbed his head at the side of the mudbath and ambled off like a rugby forward emerging from a scrum on a wet day.

Such an animal retains all his native cunning. Indeed, he seems more sensitive than ever to the sounds and scents that surround him. The merest crackle of vegetation claims his interest.

Another stag, patrolling at dusk, caught a stray whiff of my scent. He stood for a while beside a shrub. I recall that he looked like a gorilla, an effect produced by the dark face contrasting with the deep, lightly toned forehead. The stag began to move around me, keeping his distance. He was trying to localize the source of the odour. I saw him stop from time to time to lick his muzzle, which would improve the scenting capability. The stag's neck was well stretched, which meant that the mane, stiff with mud, protruded from him like a dirty ruff. When he was receiving the full force of my scent, he moved haughtily away.

Once I had an enjoyable evening's sika-watching without seeing a single animal. A friend with a parabolic reflector and powerful recorder accompanied me to a favourite ground. When night came the almost full moon compensated for the loss of sunlight, but the area where the deer grazed was thick with mist.

This fact did not deter my friend, who cleverly adjusted his equipment so that the reflector was lined up with a fine stag. We were astonished how protractedly vocal he was, most of the sounds being too quiet for us to hear unaided. The miscellany of calls included wavering notes, bleating notes, morse-like pips, leading up to the shrill whistling – a sound clearly detected without headphones. Heard in the distance the whistles might have been made by a northern Pan.

Another time, stationed near a conifer wood, I sat for well over an hour before the first deer came into view. A hind scanned the open ground for minutes on end until she was satisfied that all was well. Perhaps the presence of half a dozen hares, all grazing happily, persuaded her it was safe to move. She emerged, with other hinds in train, advancing across the grassland to feed.

I had already heard a stag whistling in the wood. Now he revealed himself, his lightly toned horns standing out against the murk. He, too, advanced, and he made for one of the hinds, but she was not ready to be served and slipped away, coquettish in her behaviour. So he turned his attention to a young stag that appeared. The proprietorial stag raised his head, the chin jutting out and the antlers almost tickling his back. When this threat gesture failed to impress the young stag, he ran bleatingly towards the newcomer. And the stranger fled.

Sika are fairly tolerant of rivals. I see the stags sparring in early spring, just before the antler fall, but this behaviour seems little more than play. When an old stag has cast, but his young retainers are still in horn, he sometimes rears up on his hind legs

Jetty on Inchcailloch, Loch Lomond. The island is a nature reserve.

A roe deer. The smallest, most graceful of Britain's native species of deer.

Inveraray Castle, which was seriously damaged by fire in 1975.

West Highland sheep. When many districts were converted to sheep-walk, large numbers of people were driven from their native glens.

The red fox. The new conifer forests provide it with abundant cover, and – in the early stages of growth, when voles are common – with much food. Hunting the Highland fox has not been ritualized as in Cumbria or the Shires. The dozing fox (*below*) is a captive animal.

A hen salmon. Fish following the River Etive enter an ingenious lift and are released from it in Loch Awe.

The head of Loch Etive and the glen wandering towards Rannoch Moor.

West Highland drovers' route, now a pleasant footpath near Kinloch Hourn.

Oban auction mart's impressive array of pens. This mart handles many cattle from the Highlands and islands.

The foot of a roe, adapted for use as the headpiece of a Highland stick.

Three roe heads from Argyll. The animals were shot not far from Loch Etive.

Highland antlers used as a coat rack at a 'Big Hoose'. Many antlers which remain undiscovered by man are chewed by the deer.

The waters of the Sound of Jura near Oban, pounding on the basalt rocks on Seil Island. Scarba Island can be seen on the horizon.

and offers them the view of threshing forelegs. The 'pecking order' in the deer world is being established throughout the year as the animals try to assert themselves.

Only once have I seen an energetic fight that lasted for more than the customary few minutes devoted to sparring. Some hinds had been disturbed and left the woods in which they were being herded by a big stag. A young eight-point stag joined them as they returned to the wood. Here the young stag came face to face with the master.

It was on an autumn day to remember. The bracken glowed brown or copper in the sunlight. Thorn trees were sheened with scarlet now that the berries had ripened. The air was tinglingly fresh. I first became aware of the antagonism between stags when I heard a bleating sound beyond a line of thorns. I moved in time to see the master advancing on his rival. He offered a threat gesture, but the stag held his ground.

During the ensuing fight, they ignored all but themselves. At one stage they were caught up in a thicket of thorn, and one of them emerged from the tangle about ten yards from where I was standing. The battle between stags was quickly resumed.

In due course, the young eight-point stag gave way. Normally he would have run off down the slope to the burn, but extreme weariness had overtaken him. He stood in the water, which was a khaki soup from peat in suspension, and his body steamed. When he had mustered the last reserves of energy, he went off among the trees.

No one can say precisely when a stag will call – when his three whistles (sometimes four) will make the gloaming tremble. When a sika gives voice, the sound does not seem loud but has great carrying power. A hind in season makes bleatingly towards him and is mounted, maybe several times in rapid succession.

Humans may think that in autumn the year is declining. But October into November is the beginning of a new year for the sika deer in the woods and for red deer on the hills. . .

5

Around Loch Awe

I was delayed between Inveraray and Cladich by a hundred thousand rainbow trout. At least, their owner assured me that was the number. The ponds in which they lived looked still and sterile, a point on which I was about to comment when a boy spread a handful of brown pellets across the water; it foamed as a few hundred trout jostled each other for food.

An elderly man ignored a sign that asked visitors not to tamper with the fish, a reasonable request. This trout 'tickler', rediscovering the joys of a distant boyhood, overbalanced and found himself knee-deep in water.

A heron circled above the brown river and tinted trees. The knots of eager trout-feeders discouraged this bird, which flew off, doubtless to return for a fish supper in the quiet of dusk.

Resuming my journey, I reached the highest point of the road between Lochs Fyne and Awe. Now I scanned a tousled, colourful landscape, the type of which Walter Scott must have been thinking when he wrote:

> Land of brown heath and shaggy wood,
> Land of the mountain and the flood.

The nearest woodland was rather prim, not shaggy. Acres of conifers stood in rows, with clumps of heather at their feet. In contrast with the new plantation was a group of birches, which looked positively unkempt.

The Campbells, proud of the extent of their western territories, declared that it was a far cry to Loch Awe. Their clan cry was "Cruachan", derived from the illustrious ben I now saw beyond Loch Awe. The ben had a grey pocket – a concrete dam at the mouth of a corrie where water is impounded for a hydro-electricity scheme.

The castle of Kilchurn occupied its islet with all the assurance of long association. It was founded in the fifteenth century, being greatly enlarged during the Jacobite troubles, when the Breadalbane Campbells stationed men here to watch the movement of people through the area.

In 1888, the Colquhoun family lived on the island, occupying a three-apartment house specially built beside the castle walls for a keeper. Mr Colquhoun was also a quarryman, and rowed across the loch each day to the quarry which supplied granite setts for the streets of Glasgow. His wife guided tourists round the castle; their four children rowed across the lake each day to attend school in Dalmally.

I culled this information from a history of Lochawe – the village, that is – which had run into four editions by 1975. It was prepared as an entry in a village history-book competition organized by Scottish Women's Rural Institutes. Information given by an elderly lady, Miss Sarah Colquhoun, included the story of the four children I have mentioned having whooper swans as pets. Descendants of those birds still fly southwards from the breeding grounds on Iceland and winter in Pike Bay.

The writer of the Lochawe history noted: "It seems strange to hear from Miss Colquhoun how these great wild birds would come ashore at the castle to be embraced by her sister, and how they recognized the Colquhoun boats when they rowed upon the loch and never made a vicious attack on them as they sometimes did on hapless fishermen and travellers." In those days, boat traffic was extensive.

> Every man had his rowing boat to fish for salmon and brown trout and to visit his friends up and down the loch; the folk beside Loch Awe almost had a Venetian existence. A young man thought nothing of courting a girl five or six miles down the loch, rowing there and back at the end of his day's work. Similarly, it was a regular thing for the plumber, the joiner and the carpenter to row back and forth across the loch in the course of their work on distant houses.

Loch Awe is long, broad and winding. Looking at a map, a stranger would expect to see this great body of water outflowing at the foot of the loch, near Ford. Yet the surplus water feeds the River Etive. Water from areas up to fifty miles away tumbles into Loch Awe, a name that was once rendered 'Lochow'.

The road I followed to the south of the loch lay in a seemingly endless green-and-brown aisle. I knew the loch was near, but a few million conifers screened it from me for most of the way. I returned by the northern route, through Inverliever, the oldest of Scotland's state forests. Here at least the trees were of various ages, and the road ran high above the loch, offering some spectacular views. This road dates from just after the 1939–45 war, and before the first gravel track was laid the foresters had to go to and from their work by boat.

One forester mentioned the return of the capercaillie. A bird had been seen some three years before, and two cocks joined blackcock at a *lek* in spring. Capers thrived in the pine woods beside Loch Awe over 200 years ago. Sir Duncan Campbell had one caught, and despatched to the King. He was in his bed-chamber when the turkey-sized bird was produced and, not having seen a capercaillie before, he was entranced.

The caper became extinct in Scotland about 1770. The changes in its preferred habitat had been too violent, and hunting pressures too great. Seventy years later, a move was made to reintroduce into the Highlands the largest and most impressive member of its grouse family. The Breadalbanes of Taymouth Castle were associated with the bird's reintroduction; they had some birds collected in Sweden and released in the Tay valley about the year 1837.

I followed two of the trails through Inverliever forest; the few capercaillie escaped my attention, though, taking a tip from a forester, I kept a sharp eye on the sky and was rewarded by seeing a golden eagle.

The Gaelic name of the capercaillie is said to mean 'horse of the woods', possibly an allusion to a clicking sound that is part of its springtime repertoire of unusual sounds. I prefer the name 'cock of the woods' (hardly anyone mentions the female!). The cock bird is dark in tone but with a green sheen to the breast and a white mark on the shoulder. The hen is appreciably smaller and rather rusty in colour. I remember seeing one perched on a young pine one quiet, sunny evening. The 'fire' in the sunlight emphasized the rusty coloration.

A forester told me about the Soay sheep – a small group kept in a fenced-off area. The sheep are derived from the old St Kildan stock. He also spoke about wildcats, which den among rocks and make regular rounds of the forest looking for small mammals as food.

Another man had the pelt of a wildcat. This was no fusion of the wild and domestic strains, or simply a domestic moggie gone wild and rough. The coarse hair sticking out from this pelt lacked lustre. The beastie's ears were short. Rings of dark hair adorned the tail. It was a true wildcat.

Museum experts, studying skeletons and skins, determine the purity of the breed by reference to such fine points as the angle of the eye sockets. In the wild, the cat manages for most of the time to stay away from man's attention. Sometimes one is caught in a trap set for a fox. A tom cat recovered from a snare left for foxes had a length of three feet. It weighed 15 pounds!

The islands of Loch Awe have been drenched by rain – and folklore. Much of the latter is fanciful. We do know that Fraoch Eilean (sometimes known as Frechelan) and Inchconnel had castles. Inishail (or Innishaile) was the site of a nunnery. Or do we know? I have read so many differing accounts. What do you make of the story of Fraoch and Mego (or Meve)? Fraoch was a 'bobby-dazzler', his hair black and glossy as a raven's feathers, his skin fairer than the snow. We have no catalogue of the features of the damsel Mego, but one version of the story relates that she loved Fraoch. He had no special love for her.

Mego, anxious to draw attention to herself, feigned ill health, telling Fraoch that the only cure was to taste the fruit of a rowan that grew on the island now called Fraoch Eilean. Witches feared the power of rowan, but this dislike was not general among other creatures. A major snag facing Fraoch was the presence of a dragon.

The lad managed to reach the island and grab some berries before the dragon was aware of his presence. Now the peevish Mego actually craved for the tree itself. He must rip it up by the roots! With commendable patience and fortitude, Fraoch did this, but as he swam back to the mainland, towing the tree, he was overtaken by a dragon. They fought to the death. Mego, fickle lass, died of shock.

The island is now well cared for, and modern excavation has

brought to light a stone carving of a running hare. Rabbits ran here in the eighteenth century. A writer about local agriculture in 1798 noted: "The only rabbits on the continent of Argyllshire are in a small island in Lochow, used as a warren by the Duke of Argyll." John Hay Allan, writing about Loch Awe in 1822, remembered in particular the gulls, "which hold the island in joint tenure with a water-eagle who builds annually upon the top of the remaining chimney". The "eagle" was an osprey; it was present here in 1833 but absent in 1859. Ospreys had nested on the castle of Kilchurn.

Of all the past inhabitants of this district, I would most liked to have met Sir Duncan Campbell – he who sent a capercaillie to the King. Sir Duncan died in 1631 and was remembered for his interest in forestry and wild creatures. In 1615 he introduced "fallow deir" to Innishaile, where today only the brambles run riot.

One day I must find time to write about 'How the West was Won by Tourists'. There is evidence of the tourist boom around Loch Awe. Tourism began to thrive with the publication of Queen Victoria's Highland journal and, locally, was accelerated in the 1870s when a single-track railway was laid between Stirling and Oban. Passing through Glen Orchy, it skirted the head of Loch Awe, where a station was established. From a pier operated the steamer *The Countess of Breadalbane*; she carried goods and passengers round the loch.

The *Countess,* originally operated by the Caledonian Steam Packet Company, was not the first steamer on Loch Awe. A vessel with a timber hull, *Queen of the Lake,* preceded her, but *Countess* became the best known and loved of the craft that furrowed the lake; she was dismantled as recently as 1953 and taken to the Clyde. The *Lochawe* came into her own on the day 'The Games' were held at Oban. She made an early morning run from a pier at Ford to the loch's northern end, and disembarking passengers were then able to board a special train to Oban.

There is a time when you are too near Ben Cruachan to appreciate the hill. I drew into a park beside the lake as excited groups of visitors were queueing for a mini-bus that would take them to the heart of the hill to see man's engineering wizardry – the works connected with hydro-electric power.

Water lapping behind the dam on Ben Cruachan is intended to feed turbines which, during the day, supply electricity into the grid. The process is reversed at off-peak times, when the turbines use surplus power received from the stations of the South of Scotland Board and drive water from the loch to the dam, pumping it to a world record height of 1,200 feet. On the following day, the water flows back down the hill, via the turbines.

I shared a sandwich with the gulls and watched a family party of ravens circling a high crag. The birds, uniformly black against a grey sky, displayed wedge-shaped tails, and the primaries were widespread, so that the wings appeared to have dark fingers. All the birds engaged in an aerobatic display, soaring, circling, swooping, climbing again.

The raven, a sacred bird to the Norsemen, was later to acquire an aura of menace. And so did the Pass of Brander, "an evil place that so straight and so narrow was". I have plucked this line from an eighteenth-century poem describing a battle in which Robert the Bruce trounced the army of John of Lorne.

At the chilling Pass of Brander, hills sweep directly into the loch where it overflows. So little level ground exists that the builders of a modern road put part of it on concrete stilts. No one is encouraged to dawdle, there being a shortage of parking places. The motorists have short but vivid impressions – of dark water, a hill with fan-shaped screes, relict tracts of oakwood, odd patches of grass where graze some adventurous sheep.

Not until 1770s was the river bridged – and even then the first attempt was hindered by a flooded river, which demolished three of the emerging arches. Drovers of cattle moving from the islands and the mainland of Argyll to the trysts knew, before the bridge was made, that fording the river was certain for but a short time in summer.

A barrage has been slung across the outflow to the loch; it incorporates a fish lift for salmon. An angler bemoaned that since the barrage was made, the river has been "nae sae guid", and that years ago fish exceeding a weight of 50 pounds were landed.

The Fishery Board has the use of a salmon hatchery established near Inverawe House; a hatchery with accommodation for three million eggs. Fish trapped at the barrage are kept in ponds until they are 'ripe', when the hen fish are stripped of their eggs. These, fertilized by dashes of milt from the cock fish, are then hatched out in special containers. The salmon fry are introduced to tributaries of the Awe, so conditions are by no means as bad as the angler led me to believe.

Each autumn, the backs of salmon break through the frothing water as they fight their way up the Awe. This is one of the short, lively rivers of the west, so unlike the long and languid watercourses of the east. Years ago, men netted the fish from boats moored at the mouth of the river. Two men crewed each boat and they slept in a bothy ashore, taking the salmon to market by boat. Stake-nets were also popular. Today a salmon sets a course between the hooks used by anglers. Incidentally, only 20 per cent of Scottish salmon fall to the anglers; the remainder are claimed by the netsmen of commercial interests, mostly in the east.

The road I followed began to descend towards Loch Etive. I found my first road victim, a dog fox slain by a motorist. Judging by the sharpness of the fox's canine teeth, it was a young animal and therefore expendable. Foxes vary considerably in tone between the extremes of red and grey, and this fox was reddish.

In parts of England, foxes are slain as part of a ritual involving many hunt supporters. Most of the hunts are mounted. In Cumbria, Wordsworth's county, however, men have for long trudged after foxes with packs of hounds. Highland foxes appear to be disposed of without fuss. The modern forester counts the fox as friend – for it dines on voles – but he keeps down the population for the sake of being a good neighbour to the sheep farmer.

Occasionally I derive amusement from reading a song written by Duncan Ban MacIntyre, a Gaelic poet, in which he lauds the fox for its depredations among the flocks. The poem, written at the time of the Coming of the Sheep by a man who preferred the old way of life, loses style through being translated into English:

> My blessing be upon the foxes, for that they hunt the sheep –
> The sheep with the brocket faces that have made confusion in all
>   the world,
> Turning our country to desert and putting up the rents of our lands.
> Now is no place left for the farmer – his livelihood is gone;

Hard necessity drives him to forsake the home of his fathers.
The township and the shielings, where once hospitality dwelt,
They are now nought but ruins, and there is no cultivation in the
    fields.
Deeply do I hate the man who abuses the foxes,
Setting a dog to hunt them, shooting at them with small shot.
The cubs, if they had what I wish them, short lives were not their
    care.
Good luck to them, say I, and may they never die but of old age.

I drove into Taynuilt. The Wordsworths associated this village with good lodgings and food. Dorothy, chilled and with a headache, warmed herself at a fire made in the sitting-room. The first meal consisted of eggs, preserved gooseberries and cream, cheese, butter and oatcakes.

The visitors were faring better than the ordinary Highland family of that period, to whom oatmeal was the monotonous mainstay of the diet. In winter, hunger pangs were alleviated, but the appetite not truly satisfied, by salted herring and pickled meat.

Taynuilt's first building was 'the house by the burn', from which the name is derived. The village spread itself over a raised beach overlooking Loch Etive. Water spreads over the lower fields at flood-time, when the River Awe in spate meets a high tide in the loch.

A farmer told me he had watched seals swimming in an area where he normally grows cereals!

6

Mysterious Etive

We went fishing, far up Etive. My friend switched off the
outboard engine; it died with a splutter. Now the only regular
sound was the lapping of water against a varnished hull.

We surveyed the still mysterious upper stretch of the loch. No
roads have so far been cut into the rocky hillsides. We felt to be
in a sterile world until a group of red deer broke a distant
horizon, moving in line-ahead formation, rather like a row of
cut-outs at a shadowgraph.

The hills do not appear to crowd the water. Ben Cruachan was
blocking part of the sky, its turrets carrying rather more snow
than was visible on the other side. I wondered to what extent the
shape of Ben Cruachan had altered since, long ago, there was a
change in the sea level and water flooded into the major part of an
ancient glen to create what is now called Loch Etive. Glen Etive,
the unflooded portion, extends from Kinlochetive to the edge of
Rannoch Moor, which it joins under the frosty stare of Buchaille
Etive Mor.

The glen has vivid memories for me – of water creaming over
great rocks, a white garron grazing in a croft near a sporting
lodge, and a blackcock perched at the top of a young larch that
swayed but did not break under the big bird's weight. Plus, of
course, the red deer.

If you feel fanciful, you will be in the mood to hear the story of
an Irish girl called Deirdre who was being pestered by the king
of Ulster when she and her lover, Naisi, decided to flee to
Scotland. Glen Etive's woodland was their first refuge. They
were lured back to Ireland and their death by the treacherous
king. In this old story is an echo of Celtic days. That mysterious
group of authorities known as 'they' associate Glen Etive with an
early Celtic saint, Fillan. 'They' could be right.

You will recall that a friend and I went fishing. I leaned over the gunwale of the boat and dipped my hand into the loch so that I could collect some water and test a story I heard at Taynuilt that Etive's upper reach has had its salinity much reduced by the flow of fresh water from some 500 square miles of country. The upper loch has been known to freeze over in winter. There was a slight hint of salt – not sufficient to flavour potato crisps! Into Loch Etive flow the Rivers Etive, Kinglass, Liever, Noe, Awe and countless burns.

Twenty miles of water extend from Kinlochetive to the point where the loch opens its mouth to the mild breezes sweeping up from the Firth of Lorne, but two great sills of rock check the salt-water flow, breaking the back of the tides. The first sill, at Connel Ferry, reduces the height of the waves by a half, and water creams and swirls and bubbles at what are known as the Falls of Lora. Was the name 'Etive' derived from these falls? *Eite* is said to mean 'raging'. The second sill of rock, off Bonawe, does not allow the sea regularly to replenish salt water in the area beyond.

As far as I know, Loch Etive has no tales of water monsters, but I was prepared to believe that they exist when I saw a grey blob on the water. My stare was returned by the large, moist, unblinking eyes of a common seal, one of an estimated thirty seals living in the loch. The head, with its eyes set forward for binoculared vision, was covered with fur which had silvery highlights.

A second seal appeared, then a third. Encircled, we reeled in the fishing lines and changed our occupations. Now we were watchers of seals, more precisely 'firth' or 'harbour' seals which are quite common in the Firth of Lorne and Loch Linnhe. Common seals surface in Loch Leven to scrutinize the tourist traffic in its headlong rush towards Fort William.

The common seal is appreciably smaller than the Atlantic or grey seal. This solemn inhabitant of outer waters is frequently seen basking on the rocks of islands. The common seal is not noticeably a sun-worshipper, indeed, and seems to enjoy lying in the rain!

Grey seals drop their pups about November, the stormy end of the year, when big seas boom against the north-west coastlines. North Rona is a large maternity area, but the nearest breeding grounds to Loch Etive are possibly those of the Treshnish Islands, beyond Mull. Hundreds if not thousands of grey seals come together for calving.

The common seal parts with its calf in late summer on a quiet part of the shore, where no other seals may be present. Both mother and offspring will float off a sandbar when the tide flows, and the common seal pup sheds its silky white coat in quick time. Cow and pup return to the coastline at feed times. The pup relies on its mother's care and milk for about two months.

Seals appear awkward, shapeless, when drawn up on the shore like so many bladders of lard. They are in their true element in water. Years ago I joined a cruise from Oban to the Seal Islands. The water off Oban was dead calm, but further out – clear of the sheltering islands – we took some of the force of an Atlantic swell and the boat periodically left the water, to rejoin it with such a smack I expected the timbers to part.

Conditions were calm again in the lee of the seal rocks. The animals that lumbered awkwardly into the water at our approach were then seen moving through the clear sea like animated torpedoes, trailing bubbles of air. The seals played around the boat with power and grace.

Our highest count in upper Loch Etive was five seals. We returned to Taynuilt without a fish to show for our efforts. That afternoon, at a slipway not far from Oban, I had another encounter with the common seal.

He was late for the appointment. The seal should have appeared at 4.30 p.m., give or take a few minutes, but now the time was almost 5. I stared across a shallow bay looking for an object that was dark, about the size of a football – the head of our truant seal.

The loch was choppy, a dozen shades of grey, and a few clouds crossed over drawing behind them a smudgy train of vapour. The passing storm set up a turbulence of air and water.

I suppose that the seal had an excuse for being late. Minutes before I arrived, a small craft with an outboard engine had buzzed across the water with the stridency of a circular saw. To a creature as sonic-sensitive as the seal, that boat's progress must have been a torment. Soon, mercifully, the boat was out of sight behind a headland.

My companion on the slipway carried a bucket half full of fish. We scanned the bay until our eyes were ready to pop. The missing seal was known to spend a good deal of time in the shallows.

We first saw the seal when he was about 200 yards away; he beheld us with cold eyes. I heard from my companion that the seal was found draggled and exhausted in a tangle of weed, the weight of the animal being a mere 14 pounds The seal's mother must have been shot.

Attention and good food restored to the seal his good looks and spirits, though having fish placed in his mouth at regular intervals seemed to have robbed him of an interest in seeking food. The common seals of Loch Etive were living on fish and crustaceans of their own catching; our seal was dependent on the man who arrived at the slipway twice daily with buckets of food.

We discussed the prospects. The shallow bay was not one of the regular seal haunts, so the chances of the orphan pup meeting up with other seals was remote. The day before I visited the slipway, the seal did not take a full meal.

His progress to the shore was slower than usual because two figures, not the customary one, occupied the slipway. The man spoke softly, soothingly, and the seal – recognizing his voice and general deportment – arrived in the shallows and began to hitch himself ashore. His body stiffened at the approach of the man, for a few thousand years of evolution had taught his kind to be wary, but the man continued to speak. He reached out to caress the seal, taking hold of him by the neck. The seal's half-hearted struggles ended when the man had lifted the animal into his arms. A quiet voice, and familiar routine, overrode the seal's native fear.

When the seal had been placed on an elevated spot at the head of the slipway, I was able to see those fine points of appearance which are not readily observed in the wild – a firm body, moist and lustrous; steel-blue but lightening in tone as the fur began to dry out. The body was finely mottled.

That day the menu for the seal included one item – herring, a few fish bought at a local shop and kept in a deep-freeze. I was told that vitamin B had been added to compensate for the loss of this vital element in the freezing process. The man broke fish into several pieces before offering food to his charge; he also carefully removed the swim bladder. The seal ate all but one of the fish, and resolutely ignored the last even though it was placed against his mouth. Enough is a feast!

The now trusting animal was carried to a simple shelter, in which it would spend the night. The seal hitched his way under cover, but stopped to growl a few times when I put a hand near him. Next morning he would be carried to the edge of the bay and released.

The main road from Taynuilt to Oban takes its time before running close to the shore. For part of the journey I travelled in an aisle between stands of brooding conifers. This made the scene at the edge of the loch all the more brilliant. Mull appeared to view through a gap at the mouth of Etive; the hills of Mull had a fiery baptism as volcanoes flared some 50 million years ago, yet today the island is green and pleasant, with woods and productive farms.

The Etive narrows were framed by a latticework of metal which is a bridge of cantilever design. The structure was pieced together early this century when the Callander and Oban railway sent out a branch to Ballachulish. The railway was opened in 1903, and now steam-hauled trains raised the echoes as they clattered high above the Falls of Lora. Beyond lay the Achnacree peat moss where, it was noticed, the line sank as a train passed over, rising gently when that train had moved on. The Ballachulish line, which ran near the sea for most of its length, was closed in 1966.

The big bridge has been modified to take motor traffic. Traffic lights ensure there is a single line of vehicles at a time. Red, amber and green: the colours which usually denote urban areas now glow above the Falls of Lora, amid Highland grandeur.

I scanned the Falls. A shag needed all its muscular strength to maintain its position at the edge of the creaming turbulence. A red-breasted merganser cruised in quieter water. Further away, long-nebbed curlew were probing at the inter-tidal mud.

The ubiquitous hooded crow was in view. One bird picked up a shellfish and dropped it on some rocks; the shell did not break. I was told that some crows use the nearby road as an anvil. It was believed that one of them deliberately placed a shellfish so that it would be shattered by the wheels of passing traffic!

The expression on the man's face indicated he did not intend to be taken seriously.

7

Highland Beef

St Columba, who used the island of Iona near Oban as a springboard for evangelical work among the northern tribes, did not like cattle – or so it was said. Columba asserted that where a cow was found, so might be found a woman; and where a woman was found, there was trouble!

I thought of the saint's irrational objections to cattle when, visiting Oban auction mart, I watched a young woman clad in jumper and jeans clamber into one of the pens. This 'tomboy' quickly appraised the quality of the cattle. Then she had some terse verbal tussles with the men about the merits and short-comings of the stock.

Most of the pens were as yet empty; they stretched away to the middle distance like an immense timber yard, and beyond them lay Oban itself with its dominating feature, McCaig's Tower, commonly and irreverently known as McCaig's Folly. Empty, too, were the sale rings where auctioneers intone like high priests at religious festivals as cattle, product of the highlands and the islands, come under the hammer. A wooden partition had been so frequently daubed by marking fluids of various colours it was like some futuristic painting.

As a layman, I stood little chance of working out the parentage of breeds and crosses of cattle that jostled in the pens. They were mainly beefers – and apparently regarded as so much protein on the hoof.

In contrast, the Highland cattle I had seen in a field near Loch Etive were instantly recognizable as such. These pure-bred animals were of medium scale, blocky, clad in tawny-red hair and with impressive horns. They looked fearsome, but were docile. Several of them stared at me from beneath fringes of coarse hair. So Scottish did they look that their owner should receive a letter of commendation – if not a subsidy – from the tourist board for keeping them here.

Man cannot resist interfering with the breeding patterns of livestock. That morning's newspaper informed me that a Lincolnshire farmer had crossed Maggie, a Highland cow, with a yak called Dalai! He hoped to create a new breed – one that would thrive, with little attention, on the wild upland pastures of Britain. Will the yakow ever reach the sale rings at Oban and be paraded before its discriminating patrons?

The Oban Times reported that Thomas Corson and Company had begun their annual October sales with the disposal of 987 calves from the islands and mainland areas north of Loch Etive.

> Select quality bred blue grey and cross Highland heifer calves suitable for future breeding met keen competition, and sold readily, but little or no interest existed in this section for the smaller, plainer heifer calf. Strong Hereford and Angus cross bullocks made prices comparable to the earlier markets. Smaller calves were cheaper, with plainer kinds very difficult to sell.

These sales were taking place against yet another national slump in prices.

If St Columba truly disliked cattle, he would have found life in the Highlands intolerable, for it was based on a cattle economy until the Coming of the Sheep swept away the old-style life and social structure. At one time a man's wealth might be assessed by reference to the number of cows he owned. A sixteenth-century chief was reported to have 1,000 beasts. A century later, a west coast chief must have been moderately pleased with sixty.

Cattle, like the people, lived at a subsistence level. The land was generally poor, the climate unhelpful, and money scarce. Only a few animals could be over-wintered, and so the surplus stock had to go, if they had not already been taken by cattle thieves. Raiding the summering stock of the neighbours was once a Highland pastime.

Continental strains of cattle now being imported into Britain are gigantic, standing at the height of a man, with the flesh hanging on them. A typical old-time West Highland cow would look poor and scraggy by comparison. Many cows were not expected to calve every year. At times the owner and his friends had actually to lift an emaciated animal from the outbuildings after a long winter.

Salvation came with the summer flush of grass on the hills. The poor, overworked acres at home were rested, or devoted to crops, for those few months when it was possible to graze the high pastures. Superstition was rife. The first day of May, known as Beltane, was devoted to driving animals around a hilltop fire to keep them from harm during the ensuing year. A man might be seen to break up a bannock and toss some of the pieces over his shoulder. He was appeasing the predators, foxes and eagles. The cattle and their progeny were brought home on the first of November, which was known as Samhain.

Cattle were then in their best condition – yet a bullock might weigh a modest 25 stones. Cattle paid the Highlander's rent and gave him sufficient monetary return for his efforts to enable him to purchase items he could not produce at home.

The cow yielded milk, some of which could be converted into butter and cheese. It is recorded that when both cattle and people were living dangerously near the starvation line, the owner might draw some blood from a barren cow as it began to thrive on the sweet grasses of early summer. Such blood, mixed with meal, provided the family with a wholesome dinner.

The great droving trade with England began with the simple economic necessity of disposing of surplus cattle. Each autumn, hundreds, then thousands, of cattle were driven to the lowland trysts and were taken from here to the booming markets of England. Argyll was regularly sending cattle to the Lowlands as early as the sixteenth century. Incidentally, from 1745 onwards, a Mr Birtwhistle – who lived in my home town of Skipton, in Yorkshire – visited the Highlands to buy cattle. He was a brave man, for then the region was aflame with Jacobite fervour. He must have needed to carry a huge sum of money, but there is no record that he was molested.

The Highland stock was brought down to Yorkshire in easy stages and exhibited for sale on Great Close, a pasture of 732 acres on Malham Moor. As many as 5,000 head of cattle at a time were assembled here, at an elevation of 1,000 feet above sea level.

Hurtley, a local schoolmaster with a taste for recording local history, informs us that when the cattle were a little freshened after their long journey, "notice was dispersed amongst the neighbouring markets and villages that a fair would be held in this field on a particular day; and lots being separated by guess as nearly as could in such manner be done to the wants and wishes of any purchaser, so much was fixed immediately by the eye upon that lot, or so much per head taking them as they accidentally were intermixed upon an average". Can you follow it?

Hurtley himself wrote that to a stranger "this mode of bargaining will appear exceedingly difficult and precarious; but it is amazing with what readiness and exactitude persons accustomed to the business ascertain the value even of a very large lot, frequently of several hundred together. As soon as these were disposed of, a fresh drove succeeded, and besides sheep and horses, frequently in great numbers".

One summer, Mr Birtwhistle marshalled 20,000 head of cattle, "every head enticed from their native soil and ushered into these fragrant pastures by the pipe of an Highland Orpheus". The tradition of importing Scottish stock was also evident at Ribblehead, another high Pennine district, in the eighteenth century. In June of 1792, a traveller found one of the two annual fairs for 'Scotch cattle' in progress there. He reached

a public house – call'd Grierstones, the seat of misery, in a desert; and tho' (unluckily for us) fill'd with company, yet the Scotch fair held upon the heath (there I go to meet Macbeth) added to the horror of the curious scenery: the ground in front crowded by Scotch cattle and drovers; and the house cramm'd by the buyers and sellers, most of whom were in plaids, fillibegs, etc

The drove routes of Scotland formed a pattern on the landscape like the pattern of veins on the back of a leaf. Stock from the coast of Argyll and its adjacent islands travelled (or was driven!) by way of the old Campbell capital of Inveraray and on to Loch Lomond and the big tryst at Falkirk.

Consider the fate of a beast raised on the island of Coll. It was ferried with others to Mull, thence to Kerrera, where it was driven into the sea and directed towards the mainland. Onwards the animal went, through the Pass of Brander to Crieff or, when Falkirk became the more prominent marketing centre, by the glens of Lonan and Nant and across Loch Awe by boat.

The Coll beast's progress would be reckoned at between ten

and twelve miles a day. This allowed time for grazing at the roadside and for a halt to rest at midday. As darkness came, the cattle were found a suitable area for the night – suitable, that is, for grazing and watering – and this became known as a 'stance'. The drover's simple meal might consist of oatmeal mixed with water. He would spend the night catnapping, alert to any unusual sounds.

When, in the nineteenth century, the drovers had to make more frequent use of roads, shoes were fitted to the cattle to reinforce their cleaves against the hard surface. Each shoe was made up of two light plates.

What happened to our beast from Coll? It might have been bought by a contractor for salting down to provide stores for a naval ship. Or part of it might have become the weekly joint for a family living in one of the thrustful new industrial towns of the West Riding or Midlands. Some Scottish cattle, refreshed by grazing the sweet limestone hills of Craven, in northern England, were driven as far as Smithfield Market in London.

Droving was well established in the middle of the eighteenth century when Joseph Mitchell wrote about it; he helpfully mentions the prices paid for stock – prices that "fluctuated like the price of money on the Stock Exchange. If there was an ample harvest, a sudden rain and a plentiful crop of grass in England, or prosperous times, prices went up; in other circumstances they declined". No telegraphs were available. The shrewdest drover would buy in the local market and sell high at Falkirk. No amount of shrewdness could help a drover if disease broke out to ravage a herd.

Mitchell wrote about the sharpness of drovers when making a bargain. During the season, these rough and excitable men "rode night and day from market to market, and many a night I have been disturbed at the inns with their noisy and riotous wrangling. There were some very respectable men among them, and good judges of cattle, but as a class they were a rough set".

England's call for fresh beef was also answered by Wales and Ireland. The droving trade went into decline during the nineteenth century when it was no longer profitable to move cattle on the hoof over long distances. Farming was in the throes of revolution, as new ideas were introduced. Landowners demanded more and more rent for 'stances' or frowned on the idea of having several hundred cattle moving across their cherished acres.

From about the middle of the century, the merry tooting of locomotives proclaimed a transport revolution. Cattle taken by rail reached the market in better condition than if they had traversed half of Britain on foot. When, in 1875, freight traffic began on the Settle – Carlisle railway, for instance, a considerable number of Scottish cattle were conveyed south in the first few months of operation.

After watching the beef cattle at Oban auction mart, I spent some time 'kenning' sheep. A group of taciturn men around a pen containing three types of sheep – Cheviot, Suffolk, Jacob's – spent a quarter of an hour surveying each animal with X-ray eyes that took in the slightest flaws. All the sheep were males, which the Scotsmen called 'tips', as do the shepherds in western Cumbria.

The stocky native sheep of West Scotland were kept mainly for their milk and wool. I refer to the time before humans were cleared away and many hills became, exclusively, ranges for sheep. An old record mentions twenty-four "milk sheepes".

The newcomers were of a type of sheep known for years on the Borders. They were tough, able to outwinter on the hills, and their coming marked the start of a new age. Walter Scott met an old Argyll chief who commented: "I have lived in woeful times; when I was young the only question asked concerning a man of rank was: How many men lived on the estate – then it was, How many black cattle it could keep, but now it is, How many sheep will it carry?"

Later, I saw a man going on his rounds of the sheep while riding a horse. Once, the horse was venerated in Argyll. The Romans, venturing into what is now Scotland, heard of a tribe called the Creons, "people of the rough lands", who occupied the northern part of Argyll. Their neighbours to the south were the Epidii, "people of the horse". The Celt regarded the horse as a sacred animal. Perhaps there is a faint echo of those times in the fact that most of us find the idea of eating horseflesh repulsive!

8

The Slate Islands

On the following morning I crossed the Atlantic – without leaving the car. My chosen route ran southwards from Oban, between knobbly hills. Reaching the head of a sea loch, I saw expanses of golden weed. Oystercatchers were periodically noisy. Where the sea breeze was being deflected by a wooded ridge, a buzzard rode the upcurrent to such good effect it appeared to be hovering, as a kestrel would.

The Road to the Slate Islands – to Seil, Easdale, Luing, Torsay, Shuna – was bounded by flowery hedges. Ragwort adorned a sunny landscape that sloped gently to a sparkling sea. A peacock butterfly sunbathed in the lee of a dyke – a wall of rough stones put together without a dab of mortar. The drystone walls of the Western Highlands testify to the efforts of thousands of farmers and their men whose names we have forgotten.

A builder of dykes has no fancy equipment; he works mainly with a skilful co-ordination of eye and hand. When repairing a gap he lets his eye range fractionally ahead of the task he is performing so that he does not have to go to the trouble handling one stone twice.

Thinking back to the time when stone would be cleared from the land and heaped at its periphery, I wondered how long man had lived in western Scotland. Presumably the first human visitors were Mesolithic hunters of some 8,000 years ago; they found sanctuary in caves at what is now Oban. Remains of the Beaker Folk have been found at Kilmartin. Bronze Age man reared up groups of stones, possibly to satisfy some deep religious urge.

Raised beaches around the sea lochs would provide early families with sites for settlements. These beaches were well drained and reasonably flat. I pictured the families crouching by their fires. We build up a picture of early man's life largely by sifting through his middens, which reveal a dependence on the produce of the sea. Man, reduced to a beach-comber, collected shellfish, caught fish and would seize every opportunity of slaying a seal, the culinary jackpot.

What did he think of the limitless forests that surrounded him on three sides? Cave paintings on the Continent indicate that in those remote times man had already reached a fine sensitivity of the spirit. His sophisticated mind would people the forest with strange creatures. Presumably he hunted deer, for antlers have been found in his old settlements and in a number of caves. I could imagine the elation a family would feel when a red stag was killed, for it represented about 300 pounds of prime fresh meat. The red deer seen by the first hunters was a much larger type of animal than that forced to live on the barren hills today.

Later, man as a farmer of sorts would apply the slash-and-burn technique to the local woods, as do some jungle peoples today. He would grow crops in the ashes, and when the ground had lost its nutrition he would move on; the virgin forest retreated before him.

The road I was following dipped towards the sea. Ahead was a riverlike stretch of salt water which a local parson of 1793 called the Sound of Clachansoail. About two miles long, it "separates the parish of Kilbrandon from the continent. The sound is narrow, being no more than 80 feet over, and admits vessels of only between 10 and 20 tons burden as it is dry and passable at low water in some parts both for men and horses . . . It runs smooth and straight with a strong current and forms a beautiful canal".

Sound? Canal? This, sir, is the mighty Atlantic!

Small craft used the sound as a short-cut to and from Oban. A ferryboat plied at Clachan, and its cost was met by the landowner and by 'stents' from tenants on the isles of Seil and Luing. The last-named island is almost within caber-tossing distance of Seil.

The Atlantic Bridge commands attention. Though static, it gives the impression it is actually jumping over the water. The soaring structure dates to the eighteenth century. On the day of my visit, election posters emanating from the presses of the Scottish Nationalist Party had been placed in the circles (occuli) which cannot have structural value but do give the bridge an added style.

In the eighteenth century, men thought of either filling in the channel (a simple operation) or of bridging the water (which would be more difficult). The factor of Lord Breadalbane favoured a bridge, for he did not like the idea of closing "so beautiful a natural canal which is useful and convenient to many people passing that way with small boats".

He was right, of course. And if the channel had been closed, Seil Island would have ceased to exist as such and tourists by the thousand would never have known the delight of standing on a rainbow arch of stone high above the Atlantic.

The bridge that was proposed had to be high so that boats could continue to use the sound. Two arches were planned, but in the end a single arch was considered sufficient. In the *Statistical Account* of 1973 it was noted: "Formerly there was a ferry boat here, but lately there has been a bridge built over it consisting of a single arch 72 feet wide and 27 feet above the highest water mark."

Resting my elbows on the parapet, I saw the Atlantic flowing between wooded hillocks. It was clearly the sea, edged by tide-smoothed rocks that were draped with weed. Crows were sorting through the natural debris.

This channel is not a serious obstruction to wildlife, and roe deer have crossed it to reach Seil Island. At least, roe have been seen on the island. I suppose they could have crossed the bridge after dark!

Argyll has a moderate density of roe deer, which are arguably the most attractive of our native deer. On dry and windless evenings I went looking for them, but fallen leaves often crackled under my feet, giving them warning of my approach. In the end I decided to pick a vantage point and wait there for the deer to emerge from woodland cover. Roebucks were rarely seen; they were still recuperating from the stresses of the rut, which takes place in summer, and in late autumn the roe sheds its antlers and assumes its winter coat of long grey hairs tipped with brown. It is an unsettling time for roebucks! What I did see regularly were does and their offspring of the year.

Historically, roe deer are dwellers in the forest. Some animals manage to endure open hill conditions, even in winter. A roe does not tolerate overcrowding, its social unit being the family group. The buck has a strong sense of territory and clings devotedly to some 30 acres of ground.

Any 'guesstimation' of roe numbers is invariably on the low side. A roe that is conscious of being overlooked by a visitor freezes and takes the first chance to move silently away. Larger species of deer tend to advertise themselves; their bone-white antlers are seen from afar, but the roebuck's horns are glorified prongs, rough and cylindrical, each having three tines.

They can be terrible weapons. A friend with a captive roe reduced the deer's territory so that a number of fallow deer could be accommodated in part of the large pen. The buck soon forced a way beneath the wire netting. Advancing on a fallow buck, he killed the much larger animal through a single lunge with his antlers. No one was allowed to enter the pen occupied by the roebuck when rutting time arrived. It was decided to dart the roebuck, using a special syringe containing an anaesthetic. As he lay in a doped state, his antlers were sawn off.

Sportsmen were peeved when they found the roebuck unco-operative. Charles St John, who blasted his way through many a Highland glen, thought that the greatest drawback to preserving roe to any great extent "is that they are so shy and nocturnal in their habits that they seldom show themselves in daylight. I sometimes see a roe passing like a shadow through the trees, or standing gazing at me from a distance in some sequestered glade; but, generally speaking, they are no ornament about the place, their presence being only known by the mischief they do in plantations and crops".

The roe has changed little in size and weight over the centuries. Nature must favour an animal of this build, and certainly it can be overlooked. I had a strong feeling in Argyll that no matter where I was standing there would be a roe deer less than half a mile away. Surely, there was one within half a mile of the Bridge over the Atlantic.

Beyond the bridge I entered a bountiful landscape. On the bridge itself grew fairy foxglove, a North African species which has a flowering season from May until autumn. On Seil, a palm tree grew happily in a garden. Tufts of pampas grass were seen in their strawy autumn splendour. Montbretia was in bloom. Some Russian vine appeared to have exploded across a garden wall.

The fields that extended from roadside to sea's edge held a large number of heavy beef cattle. Beyond the sea were to be viewed the low, dark forms of headland and island. No cattle in Britain can have had a pleasanter setting. A Hereford-type bull of vast size and undoubted strength was nonetheless as docile as a favourite spaniel. A bull surprised me by sitting down on its haunches like a dog!

Luing, an island consisting mainly of two high ridges with a glen between them, has given its name to the latest of the beef breeds. The Cadzow brothers experimented with the crossing of the Beef Shorthorn and Highland cattle: the result, a commercial success. The Shorthorn strain predominates, but the animal is quick to mature.

The road across Seil Island passed over marshy ground bedecked by yellow iris. I drove up a hill beyond and found myself on a ridge from which I gazed across sheep-frequented sward. A bronze indicator was my guide to the district; the indicator was placed at the highest point of the island to commemorate the Coronation of Queen Elizabeth II.

The road ended in a world of loose slate, with a view across the sea to Mull's great cliffs, themselves slate-grey in mist. I was at Ellanbeich, with slate all around and slate tinkling under my feet.

A jetty was formed of slate. A wall of slate retained its shape because it had been swaddled in strong netting. A rustling pier, and the remains of old equipment, were more classic signs of a dead industry.

Dean Monro, a sixteenth-century visitor, mentioned the slate under the name 'skailzie'. The township was then known as Caolas, a name also employed for the sound that separated the main island from Easdale. Slate from Easdale had been used to roof Castle Stalker near Appin in the days of James IV. A generation or two later, it was also being placed on the roof of Armaddy Castle.

Ellanbeich comes from Eilean-a-beithich, or Isle of Birches, which lay in the Sound of Caolas. This two-acre plot where the birches grew was made up of the finest slate, which was removed in such quantities that eventually a hole 250 feet below sea level had been excavated. A rim of rock separated the workings from the sea.

Its precarious nature was tested several times. Then, in November 1881, an unusually high tide combined with a south-west gale. The rim of rock was shattered and the quarry was flooded. The Isle of Birches was no more.

Easdale has been reduced by quarrying to a stub-end of its former self. A woman I met told me she lived across the water. That morning she had voyaged by ferry the 200 yards from Easdale to the main island. An uneasy sea hurled spray over the gunwales.

No longer is slate quarried on Seil Island. In its latter years, the industry worked fitfully, and Balvicar closed down in 1965, snapping a long craft tradition. The quarry owners had been cursed by heavy transport costs and a shortage of skilled men.

From the pier I surveyed a jungle of weed being stirred by the tide. Across a sun-dappled sea lay the dark profiles of lesser islands. I thought of otters.

The rows of white-painted cottages built for quarry families on Seil Island are reflected in an otherwise dark lagoon, which sends the makers of Highland films into raptures. When it was decided to film Gavin Maxwell's book *Ring of Bright Water,* this area was the choice for many outdoor settings.

I first saw the film while staying on a small Hebridean island not very far from Seil. A single projector was available, and so I could chat with my neighbour between reels. When only half the first reel had passed through the projector, dozens of dark objects began to leap about on the screen, and the attendant – somewhat embarrassed – stopped the projector and removed the 'foreign bodies'. He explained they were husks from a bag of experi-mental grass seed that had somehow been mixed up with the film container in its transit from the mainland.

Ring of Bright Water was recalled again as I chatted with the ferryman at Cuan Sound, the fierce stretch of water between Seil and Luing. He mentioned the otters he sometimes saw early in the morning, when the busy world of humans was hushed.

Back on the mainland, I climbed half-way up the Hill of the Buzzards and found a couch of springy blaeberry on which I might lie as I soaked up the last of the day's sunshine. The quiet landscape induced drowsiness – until a buzzard called. It was a ringing cry, *pee-oo, pee-oo*. The buzzard rode the air on broad wings that scarcely moved; it might have been a child's kite.

The bird was in a setting that was to its every satisfaction – hill-farming country in the west, with open fields and woodlands and hills to offer a variety of food and many nesting sites. The countryfolk are now more tolerant of the buzzard than they were forty years ago when, as I recall, many a gamekeeper's gibbet held the bodies of these majestic birds. Half a dozen buzzard corpses were displayed on one gibbet I saw in a glen in East Ross-shire.

Argyll's many buzzards take advantage of large tracts of scrubland which are infrequently visited by man; the birds can nest in peace, which they prefer, being unbearably shy in the early stages of nesting.

A stalker I met said he watched a pair of buzzards from a hide he built. When the young were new-hatched, the adults seemed to develop the ability to stare straight through the hessian that covered the hide. They stayed away during the hours of his vigil. One day, however, a bird flew over the nest and actually dropped food to the nestlings. The buzzards overcame their shyness when their offspring were about three weeks old.

In autumn and winter, the buzzards of Argyll are bold to the point of impudence. They perch on telegraph poles and blithely overlook traffic passing a few yards away. Whenever I went into Oban by the road from Taynuilt, I saw three buzzards hanging about the main road, sometimes perched on posts and at other times soaring over roadside ridges.

I teased a buzzard near Loch Awe, stopping my car, which caused it to fly from its perch to a neighbouring pole, and so on for maybe half a dozen poles. Then it shook me off, taking a long, low glide that brought it back to the original pole.

And there it perched, displaying its particularly light plumage. For a moment, a telegraph pole had become a totem.

9

Benderloch and Appin

Farmers and fishermen were the denizens of Oban when William and Dorothy Wordsworth rode into town. The local boats were small, as insignificant as water-beetles as they sailed across the bay.

It was when the first steamer from the Clyde arrived puffing and panting about the middle of the nineteenth century that Oban lost its rustic character. Today, an obelisk on the island of Kerrera – which acts as a gigantic breakwater for Oban – immortalizes a man called Hutchinson who took the first steamer across to Mull. One of his workers was a bright young lad called David MacBrayne, whose name was to become synonymous with inter-island transport.

More smoke clouded the air, and more of the Oban gulls began to develop a blink, when in 1880 a railhead was established. Oban began to blossom as a tourist resort, and now it thrives on the money spent by visitors; they get good value for their outlay.

In the old days, a ferry at Connel awaited travellers who wished to cross the Etive narrows to Appin. A railway bridge was strung across the gap and, though an outstanding piece of engineering, is a preposterous adornment to the scene.

The Wordsworths thought that Connel was dreary. When they reached the shore, the ferryboat was on the northern shore. William attracted the attention of the ferrymen, but they did not rush to assist. The men were surly, indeed, and dawdled over their duties.

You may recall that the Wordsworths were using a vehicle drawn by a horse. So roughly handled was this animal by the ferrymen that he was upset for many days to come. The ferrymen drove the horse hard over slippery stones; they beat the animal as they pushed him into the boat. Naturally, the horse retaliated, stamping its hooves against the bottom-boards. Everyone in the ferry thought it would be holed. At the other bank, the bewildered and nervous animal was verbally abused and whipped ashore.

When I had crossed the bridge, I looked back and around me at the braes of Etive. They are well wooded, which was the case early in the eighteenth century when Gilfillan wrote a love song that became famous as *The Braes Aboon Bonawe*. The lovesick swain declared;

> I'll hunt the roe, the hart, the doe,
>   The ptarmigan, sae shy, lassie,
> For duck an' drake I'll beat the brake,
>   Nae want shall thee come nigh, lassie.

In the glens of old were dense stands of oak, birch, ash and alder. Pines growing on high land – trees compared in their height and bulk with those of Norway – were systematically felled around 1730 by iron-smelters from Ireland. The timber was converted into charcoal. When a Lancashire company moved in, ships from Ulverston sailed into Loch Etive with cargoes of iron ore which they discharged at a furnace established on the flats between the Rivers Awe and Nant. The ships sailed away with loads of pig iron.

Meanwhile, the tree-felling continued, and charcoal was made in vast quantities to feed the furnace. Half a dozen years after the arrival of the Lancashire company, Thomas Pennant was bemoaning that the foundry "will soon devour the beautiful woods of the country".

Now the "braes aboon Bonawe" are wooded again. I have already mentioned the roe deer which benefits from such cover. A forest ranger I met near Loch Etive reported he had seen a buck that had cast its antlers on 23 September, which he considered early. Most antlers are shed in October and November. Few of them are found by man, for they are small and inconspicuous.

A local family told me that roe soup is delicious! I agreed with them, having tasted it several times. Charles St John wrote: "I do not think that roe are sufficiently appreciated as venison, yet they are excellent eating when killed in proper season, between October and February, and of proper age. In

summer, the meat is not worth cooking, being dry and sometimes rank."

Benderloch, a district of North Lore, is basically crofting
country, and the crofters are small-holders, occupying the land
under a special form of tenancy. Proud and independent by
nature, their feelings have been jolted in recent times by the
consequences of inflation. Crofts are no longer viable. Many
crofters have become part-timers on the land, augmenting their
incomes by other work.

Benderloch is an area of dark earth, little farms, little fields, in
some of which were pikes of hay capped by fabric or plastic
sheeting to protect them from the rain. I chatted with a crofter
about the weather. Autumn is generally a bright, dry time, he
said. There is the chance of some dry weather in January and
February, May and June are reasonably good, with hot spells,
and by the end of June it's wet again!

Highland folk have for long taken a harvest from both land and
sea. Local enterprises between Etive and Creran were an oyster
hatchery producing 10 million seed-oysters a year in time, and a
seaweed-processing plant, some of the weed used being brought in
from the isles.

Loch Creran resembled Loch Etive in having a narrow stretch
across which a railway bridge could be flung to accommodate the
Ballachulish railway. A tarmac road extends round the loch.

The Creran I saw was flat calm, its water reflecting hills
bedecked by bracken and native trees. There were patches of
white in the reflection, many local houses being whitewashed.

The main impression, on looking at the hills around the loch,
was of bountiful nature. A carpet of Grass of Parnassus grew
near where I parked the car; there was also bog asphodel. Native
woodland – birch, ash, alder and a few beech – was conspicuous.
Scots pines, standing to attention, were bonneted by masses of
dark green foliage.

Wading birds scurried along the tideline. Eider, blunt-looking
sea ducks, looked quite mournful on that quiet morning. Herons
waded in the shallows.

The district of Appin is named after 'Abbey-land', a reference
to Lismore. Cattle tugged at the more succulent plants on a hill
where bracken was dying back and coming into tonal harmony

with the reddish jackets of the beasts. A Highland cow, standing
on an outcrop with its outjutting horns giving it a strong Nordic
look, was as regal as any hill stag. As I watched, the cow
stretched out to browse a thorn tree.

The presence of cattle benefits a hill. Beasts thrive on coarse
vegetation, and tug at the vegetation as they graze, unlike sheep
which graze the plants finely until there is a dense mat. The
copious droppings of cattle add nourishment to the ground,
whereas the droppings of sheep – firm and dark – are of little
value.

Appin is a pleasant land. I saw Castle Stalker dreaming in the
mist – a fine structure rebuilt for James IV by Duncan Stewart of
Appin and impressive not only because it stood on an island but
because the proportions were great. Much of the vernacular
architecture of Appin is modest in scale. I saw low, whitewashed
buildings that were roofed by corrugated iron. This iron was
painted red, though in some cases it was deeply rusted.

Port Appin had a display of late flowers, some of them
escapees from gardens that had spread joyously along the hedges.
I remember in particular the scarlet glory of fuchsia.

From the low shoreline of Loch Linnhe I beheld a cloud-
streaked Morven. Wraiths of vapour drifted half-way up its cliffs
as though the cloud had nowhere special to go. The wild goats of
Morven frequently move in a clammy greyness.

A sudden craving for strong tea and home-made scones was
satisfied by the tea-room at a now disused railway station. This
Scottish tea-room, like others I had visited, preserved a strong
Edwardian flavour. A customer does not queue at the counter but
sits at a small, invariably circular table that is draped by a cloth.
The teapots are of the old-fashioned pot variety, not of metal with
handles that become too hot to be held. And sugar arrives in a
bowl, and not in an awkward-to-open sachet.

A fishing boat, outward bound, was having an easy passage on
Loch Linnhe. A great black-backed gull flew alongside the road –
and also alongside the loch. I maintained my car speed at the pace
of the bird. That gull did not appear to be flying fast, but it was
'clocked' at 35 miles an hour!

I had seen Castle Stalker, which relies as much on its setting as
its architectural accomplishments. Now I looked at the 'big hoose'

A new road on stilts near the Pass of Brander. The route is followed by many visitors to Oban.

A new bridge over the Leven, opened in 1975, narrows near Ballachulish.

Grannie's Heeland Hame! This fine example of a thatched cottage can be seen at Plockton.

A badger on its food-hunting rounds. Some Highland badgers have been known to knock over dustbins and lick clean the tins that have contained food.

Loch Hourn, a sea loch whose inmost stretches are dominated by high hills that seem to spring directly from the water.

A Highland pony. This type of animal has for long been employed to bring slain deer off the hill.

A group of black guillemots. A Scottish name for the species is 'tystie', after its thin call.

The common gull, photographed beside a Highland loch.

West Highland red deer. This group of hinds was seen grazing in the late afternoon.

A Highland burn. Notice also the line of posts, part of a fence at a division between two marches.

Preparing for the new landscape. Rough land ploughed in advance of planting with conifers.

The new landscape – rows of conifers, mainly sitka spruce, over 400 million of which have now been planted in Britain.

The metal-framed footbridge in Glencoe.

Rounding up the sheep in Glencoe.

at Duror, a most sophisticated building with stepped gable and corner turrets in the Scottish/French fashion.

Dorothy and William Wordsworth saw the district of Duror by moonlight. Harvesters were still busy. They watched a Highlander and a small girl driving home the cow. Then, for miles, the Wordsworths saw neither man or beast – only a little evidence of human occupation. Household linen was seen bleaching beside the burns.

At a broken bridge, the Wordsworths took their horse to the water – but they could not make it cross in the accepted way. The horse bolted, leaving the vehicle behind. When local people arrived to help, William treated them to 'wee drams' at the local inn.

On the beach were 'whoodies'. One bird looked as though it might be confiding enough to allow itself to be photographed. When I stopped the car, it was airborne in seconds. I recalled seeing a hooded crow in one of the glens near Oban. The bird occupied a knoll, and watched my approach. Then it simply walked a few yards over the top of the knoll, going out of my sight. Incidentally, hooded crows were perched on the goalposts of a football pitch on the high ground above Taynuilt. Always full of curiosity, the crows flew down to investigate a plastic bag before returning to deck the horizontals of the goalposts.

The gruff voice of the crow punctuates every day. At nesting time, a pair of birds repairs to the extensive scrubland, at fairly low elevation, or selects an isolated tree higher up the hill. Outside the nesting season, the crow is gregarious. There is a winter roost of members of the crow family in Argyll where, at peak time, over 1,000 birds are present. Jackdaws are the most common birds, but rooks, hooded crows and even a few ravens turn up at this woodland dormitory.

Men have riven slate from the hill near Ballachulish for about 200 years – and their labours show. The village is dominated by heaps of slate, which are not easily colonized by plants, for these heaps must shift a good deal, especially at the thaw that follows a period of frost.

The Wordsworths remembered the area because the black-smith repaired their damaged vehicle, working at speed; he was desperate to get into the hayfield. When Dorothy suggested that much of the hay must be spoiled by the weather, he said this was not the case. High winds dried the grass quickly, and the people had such an understanding of the climate they got in the hay "with a blink". William discovered with joy that a Cumbrian presided over the works at Ballachulish.

The name of this village means "the township of the straits or narrows". It is a reference to the mouth of Loch Leven, through which the tide forces itself with a flurry of wild water. Car ferries were still operating across the turbulent strait; the water creamed as, with surging engine and spinning props, the boats fought with the tide. (The valiant ferries became redundant with the opening of a new bridge in December 1975. Like the bridge at Connel Ferry, it will become accepted as part of the scene. But will it ever look truly at home?)

A common seal, showing only its head above water, stared mournfully at the clangour on the almost completed bridge. Otters are occasionally seen in Loch Leven and from around the loch, for the otter is a great overland traveller, crossing the watersheds to well over 1,000 feet above sea level as it moves from loch to loch or river to river.

My most recent sighting of an otter had been in springtime. I stood beside a lochan edged with reeds as waterfowl began to call. A general exodus of birds began from that part of the lochan where the otter appeared, swimming with only his flat-topped head visible. Later the patrolling otter also showed the top of his back and part of his tail or 'rudder'. He was like a scaled-down Loch Ness monster. I heard his contact call – a sibilant whistle.

For over half an hour the otter swam, turning, diving, sur-facing again – brimming over with energy, and not appearing to be seriously interested in food. A friend saw a playful otter leap well clear of the water.

In the main, the otters of Argyll are sea-going; they operate from rocky shores, denning in holes that are known locally as 'hadds'. Only the guard hairs of an otter become wet through immersion; beneath these hairs is a dense, soft underfur that remains dry. A diving otter traps in its pelage a good deal of air. Bubbles stream from it like strings of transparent beads.

Alasdair Alpin MacGregor has recorded a Highland tradition that the skin of the 'king otter' has occult powers. Killing such an otter depended partly on luck, for the only part of its exterior believed to be vulnerable was a white spot under the chin – a spot no larger than a sixpence. "Tradition has it that many who followed Charlie to Culloden carried with them a tiny piece of the king otter's skin, and that this is how they escaped injury or death when swords were clashing everywhere around them. . . ."

I motored around Loch Leven and went on to Fort William. Mine host at one of the local hotels entertained his customers by playing reels on a violin. He was also proficient at the pipes.

At another hostelry, a few years ago, I descended a grand staircase at what I thought would be breakfast-time. A lady member of the staff said the meal was not yet ready. She urged me to: "Listen for the pipes!" Which pipes?

Then, from the great hall, came the stirring strains of bagpipes. Mine host, clad in Highland dress, strode up and down the hall. Guests appeared from their rooms and sleepily inquired if the Standard had been raised. Were the clans on the march once again?

The incident prompted one of them to define a Scottish gentleman as "a Scotsman who knows how to play the bagpipes – but doesn't".

Yet the skirl of a solitary piper in the hall of that large building marked out that day as one that was very special.

10

A Queen's Travels

Plumes of smoke rose above Loch Linnhe on an August day in 1847. They marked the presence of a flotilla of steamers on course for Fort William. Queen Victoria was on tour.

Her steam yacht, *Victoria and Albert,* was but five years old, being roomy and comfortable. Sir Robert Peel had arranged for the new craft to be driven by a screw propeller so that the Queen was not disturbed by the beat of paddles as they turned. Escorting the royal yacht up the sea loch to Fort William were *Black Eagle, Garland, Undine, Fairy* and *Scourge.*

Prince Albert and Victoria's half-brother Charles set off in *Fairy* to see Glencoe. They returned at 7.20 with a report of an extraordinary carriage, with a seating capability of thirty, in which they had been driven up the glen. When the local people had recognized Albert, they insisted in taking the horses from the carriage and drawing it by their own efforts. Albert thought that Glencoe was "very fine", though not quite as much so as he had expected. (It would appear that the weather was dull.)

Next morning, with the rain sheeting down, Victoria and Albert were greeted by a crowd of Highland folk. They travelled by carriage to their holiday home at Ardverikie, by Loch Laggan.

I invested £3 in a second-hand book that evoked the spirit of those days. My purchase was *Leaves from the Journal of Our Life in the Highlands,* covering the years from 1848 to 1861; it was published by Smith, Elder (Charlotte Brontë's publishers) in 1868. Originally intended for private circulation only, it was made available to the public, though the author's name does not appear on the spine and title page. Victoria dedicated her book "to the dear memory of him who made the life of the writer bright and happy".

Leaves from the Journal is an unpretentious book, quiet in tone, with simple and direct prose. Every page has about it a charm and freshness that makes an immediate appeal to the reader. The Queen did not claim to be skilled as an author; she was providing for the most part "mere homely accounts of excursions near home". Ivor Brown has written that the *Journal* is one of the happiest books ever written.

Several weeks of life in the Highlands released the Queen from the stuffiness of the London court. Her jaunts here allowed her time to spend in the company of her beloved Albert and, to a lesser extent, her children. She travelled, sometimes incognito, in wild country; she met – and enjoyed meeting – rural folk with unaffected manners.

Victoria and Albert rapidly became more Scottish than the Scots, adopting the tartan, learning Scottish dancing and, in the case of Albert, wrestling with the intricacies of Gaelic. Incidentally, Albert designed a Balmoral tartan – black, red, lavender, backed by grey. Eventually, there was tartan everywhere, even on the linoleum.

For them, everything north of the Tweed was bathed with romance. In Scotland, they did not become daily involved with political matters – though many a senior politician came to see them, huffing and puffing along the weary miles through unfamiliarly wild surroundings.

The vexing social problems of the day were no great concern at holiday-time. When Victoria saw "children with long shaggy hair and bare legs and feet" they were regarded as picturesque adornments to a street scene, rather than as urchins whose parents could not afford to provide them with footwear. Following her first visit to Scotland, Victoria wrote to Lord Melbourne that "the Highlands are so beautiful and *so* new to me".

The royal visitors faced some grim weather, and the *Journal* has frequent references to rain. There were days when mist swaddled the hills and drizzle gave the air 90 per cent humidity; neither circumstance dampened the spirit of the young queen.

She first visited Scotland in 1842, voyaging in the *Royal George* (the handsome royal yacht) which slammed into rough seas on the east coast passage. The Queen confessed to feeling distinctly unwell. Looking for the first time at the Scottish coast, however, she allowed the romance of the ocasion to flow through her mind. It was so dark, rocky, bold and wild, "totally unlike our coast". Bonfires flared on the cliffs as part of the welcome. On the deck of a small fishing boat that came out to greet them was a piper. A large steamer drew near and they saw a band that provided music to which the passengers could dance.

Bad weather delayed their arrival at Edinburgh, and when they reached the city it was swathed with fog. Yet the tour was triumphant, taking them on to Dalkeith (which was obscured by "Scotch mist"), to Perth and Scone, Dunkeld and Taymouth (with a sail on Loch Tay). At breakfast, the royal teeth closed enthusiastically on oatmeal porridge and "Finnan haddies".

They remembered with special clarity their visit to Taymouth Castle, where Lord Breadalbane assembled lusty Highlanders in the hall and beside the Gothic staircase. He also arranged for a message to be written in lamps placed in the grounds. The message proclaimed: "Welcome Victoria – Albert".

They were, as Victoria recalled, "only twenty-three, young and happy". Victoria as a young woman was very lively, forever dashing about. Albert, keen sportsman, went out from Taymouth and bagged nineteen roe deer, several hares and some pheasants. When seeking red grouse, he did not shirk the peculiar stresses of Highland sport, and at times he waded up to his knees in bogs. Three brace of grouse fell to his gun. At Taymouth, the royal visitors were interested in a wounded capercaillie being kept here. It was, wrote Victoria, a magnificent large bird. The species had become extinct in Britain, but their host, Lord Breadalbane, imported some replacement birds from Sweden. His lordship also owned some American bison.

Rain did at least make the Highland burns lively. Victoria and Albert, taken for a voyage on Loch Tay, looked across at Ben Lawers and noticed "small waterfalls descending its sides amid other high mountains, wooded here and there". The rain persisted – and so did the visitors. They went on to Drummond Castle, between Crieff and Stirling. The weather brightened. Albert was out of bed at 5 a.m. to go deer-stalking. He returned, a little before three in the afternoon, "dreadfully sunburnt, and a good deal tired". He had shot a stag.

The comparatively new sport of stalking had bitter-sweet memories for him. Writing to Charles, Prince Leiningen, Albert declared: "Without doubt, deer-stalking is one of the most fatiguing, but it is also one of the most interesting of pursuits. There is not a tree, or a bush, behind which you can hide yourself . . . One has, therefore, to be constantly on the alert in order to circumvent them; and to keep under the hill out of their wind, crawling on hands and knees, and dressed entirely in grey."

The Highland jaunts helped Victoria to face the stresses of being Queen for most of her long life. In 1844, she and Albert were at Blair Atholl, and Victoria rejoiced in the ever-changing, splendid views. Albert told her that frequent changes constituted the chief beauty of mountain scenery.

Just outside the window of their quarters was an enclosure in which two stags roared or fought. The royal visitors were taken on a pony ride to the hills, with "not a house, not a creature, near us, but the pretty Highland sheep, with their horns and black faces". A small procession was formed on deer-stalking days. Up in front was Peter Fraser (a wonderfully active man); bringing up the rear came a pony bearing a large luncheon box!

It was all so different from life in southern England. The burns were "full of stones, and clear as glass". There was "great peculiarity about the Highlands and Highlanders; and they are such a chivalrous, fine, active people". Indeed, the folk seemed more attractive the further north the royal visitors went. "Near Dunkeld, and also as you get more into the Highlands, there are prettier faces."

At Blair Atholl, Victoria saw a flight of ptarmigan, the arctic-type grouse of the hilltops. Ptarmigan still fly over the broken ground around Glen Tilt and its neighbours. She saw "plovers, grouse and pheasants", whose calls still punctuate the long summer days in that part of Scotland.

When it was clear to them that they must return again and again to the Highlands, they decided on a local home. The choice eventually was Balmoral, "a pretty little castle in the old Scottish style" (she wrote in 1848, before the ever-restless Albert had a chance to rebuild the place).

A year after they had moved into Balmoral, the diarist Greville visited them and wrote:

The place is very pretty, and the house very small. They live there without any state whatever; they live not merely like private gentlefolks, but like very small gentlefolks, small house, small rooms, small establishment. There are no soldiers, and the whole guard of the Sovereign and of the whole Royal Family is a single policeman who walks about the grounds to keep off impertinent intruders or improper characters . . . they live with the greatest simplicity and ease. The Prince shoots every morning, returns to luncheon, and then they walk or drive. The Queen is running in and out of the house all day long; often goes about alone, and walks into cottages, sits down, and chats with the old women.

Victoria lived a fairly frugal life. Disraeli, a visitor to Balmoral in 1868, dined with the household and, "between ourselves, was struck, as I have been before, by the contrast between the Queen's somewhat simple but sufficient dinner, and the banquet of our humbler friends".

Edwin Landseer first stayed at Balmoral in 1850, the year he received a knighthood. Romance as well as paint soaked the canvasses he produced. There is a study, a conversation piece, typical of his approach to Highland life – an approach that must have been similar to that of his royal patrons, for they were happy to acquire many of his paintings. Albert, clad in tartan, is seen presenting a stag to the Queen by Loch Muich. The stag is in an attractive death pose. The Prince of Wales (also in tartan) sits astride a white garron. The hills are marshalled for effect, rather like a backcloth at the theatre. Portraits by Winterhalter were also given wallspace at Balmoral.

I have indicated that Victoria's exuberance was more than sufficient to counter the grim weather that seemed to follow her around the Highlands. For instance, when lunching on Ben MacDhui she had to face a bitter wind. The Queen accepted the advice of those around her that pure water would be too chilling. She must add a little whisky to it! Climbing Lochnagar, above her beloved Balmoral, she had to face cold and misty weather. Near the top the visitors walked through "very thick fog . . . the mist drifted in thick clouds so as to hide everything not within one hundred yards of us".

The wind strengthened during the descent. Men striding ahead of the royal visitors were like ghosts when viewed in the weak light. Suddenly there was one of those transformation scenes in which the Highlands excel: they walked out of the cloying vapour and saw the low country with clarity and colour.

Albert bagged a stag in Ballochbuie and a roe in Abergeldie Woods. Other deer were disturbed when an old woman looking like a witch, and holding two immense crutches, walked through the area. Albert, firing later, slew a young blackcock.

And so it went on, through a succession of delectable autumns. When Albert died, still quite young, his widow returned – with sadness in her heart and a terrible nostalgia – to the settings in the Highlands they had enjoyed when they were young.

My thoughts about Queen Victoria began with an account of how she sailed up Loch Linnhe and disembarked at Fort William. When this trip took place, the views of Victoria and Albert about the Highlands were not yet formed. On the way north, they entered Loch Fyne. Victoria could not recall the voyage to Inveraray because she had a headache and remained below deck. She roused herself as Inveraray drew near, noticing that the undulating hills beside the loch were very green but not very high. Victoria, amateur artist, commented on the tonal ranges – the hills "splendidly lit up, green, pink and lilac".

At Inveraray they met the Marquis of Lorne, "just two years old, a dear, white, flat, fair little fellow with reddish hair, but very delicate features, like both his father and mother: he is such a merry, independent little child". At lunch, they saw Highlanders with halberds standing in the room.

The royal yacht went round Kintyre; the royal couple and their entourage were taken through the Crinan Canal in a decorated barge, drawn by three horses, ridden by postilions in scarlet. Of the features seen after leaving Oban, Victoria recalled a flat rock called The Lady's Rock on which, she heard, a McLean left his wife, hoping that she would be washed away. She was however saved before the tide could reach her.

As the royal barge entered the vaulted hall of Fingal's Cave it "heaved up and down on the swell of the sea . . . The sea is immensely deep in the cave. The rocks, under water, were all colours – pink, blue and green – which had a most beautiful and varied effect".

So to the morning when the flotilla sailed up Loch Linnhe. Victoria and Albert arose at 7.30 to find that the district was being swept by rain. It rained during the carriage trip to Ardverikie. Albert went further north, to see the Caledonian Canal, and they were in due course reunited at Fort William, from where they sailed on the following morning, crossing an uneasy sea . . .

11

Home from Home

A friend who has a sparse knowledge of architectural styles recognizes only three types of Highland home: the Big Hoose, Grannie's Heeland Hame – and the bothy!

The Big Hoose can be dour, plain, only a cut or two above a cotton mill, or a gracious and opulent structure, decked with corner turrets, looking shyly at you from behind groves of rhododendrons in which pheasants lurk. Its garden will have a deer larder of wooden slats, usually painted white. The rooms of the hoose bristle with mounted deer heads.

At one such dwelling we visited, the grounds were overrun with sheep, the 'hoose' with cats, the nearby loch with sea trout and the hill with deer. It had become a wildlife park unintentionally. The wife of the owner accorded us an honour by 'dressing for dinner', or so I thought. Within ten minutes, I established that with her long gown she had dressed against the menace of draughts. Every room was turbulent with a dozen eager, chilling currents of air. My legs lost all sensitivity below the knees.

I remember excusing myself at another Big Hoose. After asking for the 'wee hoose' – to a stunned silence – I was handed a paraffin heater and directed down a long passage, at the end of which was a room almost as large as a modern bungalow, and in one corner of which stood the toilet. I recall in particular the long walk, over wooden blocks which now were loose. I raised half a dozen blocks at each footfall and heard them click back into place as I passed.

Venturing, unbidden, into the grounds of another Big Hoose, we found ourselves in a tropical paradise. Palm trees thrived. We plucked leaves from some eucalyptus, and discovered a greenhouse that was half full of exotic fruits. When the laird appeared, my companion was soon in amiable conversation, and minutes later a bottle of whisky and three glasses had been produced; we were friends.

The second architectural style acknowledged by my friend is Grannie's Heeland Hame, a term applied to a small cottage, and especially the roofless variety. When the gaunt silhouette comes into view, my friend scans a weed-ridden path and tangle of briars. Then he mutters darkly about the Coming of the Sheep and the Depopulation of the Highlands – about the Displacement of Grannie, indeed.

Without stopping to inquire why the cottage is deserted, he fixes his eyes upon me – a Sassenach – as though I am personally to blame. I protest. The sheep that swamped the Highlands came from the Borders, I claim. The men who tended the sheep were from the same region. I also assert that, as far as I am aware, no member of my family was involved in the old outrage against the Highland Scots.

A bothy, as defined by my friend, is any building in which he spends a night or two. By implication, it is small and a little rough, though not necessarily remote. To his wife's annoyance, he insists in calling his home a 'bothy'. All bothies are the same, he booms, with "two ees (eyes) and a moo (mouth)". I hasten to add that such a building has two windows and a door set between them. When the roof space is used the fact is proclaimed by a dormer window.

I have spent a week or so in a number of Highland bothies – a type known elsewhere in the country as "rented accommodation, self-cooking". One of them was so furnished it might have just been vacated by Jacobites. The sideboard held three Amen Glasses with which to toast the King Over the Water. A round serving tray was multi-coloured, and when a plain silver tankard was placed in the middle of the tray a portrait of the Prince formed on the silverwork.

The bothy I occupied during my autumn wanderings had originally served a stalker and his family. It was typical of Victorian times, when the rise in popularity of the deer forest led to a building boom in the Highlands. This bothy was now available for visitors who had not acquired the Grand Hotel complex. It was under the care of an elderly stalker living some ten miles away, and I welcomed his visits.

He was tall, spare of frame, silver-haired, quiet-spoken (as are the folk in the west), and yet others spoke of him as one of the finest of the old-time stalkers whose patience with visitors was limitless but who used a gun on the hill with such accuracy you would swear the bullet had a homing device attached to it.

The bothy overlooked a lochan and was, in turn, overlooked by a hill. This shut off three-quarters of the sky. At dusk, the hill yielded a variety of foragers. Red deer arrived to graze the better land of the glen. At about 8.30 p.m., a crash near the back door indicated the arrival of a badger, which was fond of knocking over the dustbin and licking out food tins discarded during the day.

The bothy was not just imposed upon the countryside; it was part of it. A garron regularly scratched itself on some wrought ironwork, and sometimes it condescended to take food offered through the open window. This animal sniffed at any food for such a long time I began to think it ate through its nostrils. A robin used the highest point of an outbuilding as a perch from which to offer its soulful autumn song. Once, awaking early, I saw a red fox trotting lightly by.

Externally, the bothy conformed to my friend's ideas. It was plain to the point of being spartan, though since the last stalker and his family lived here the place had been modernized. The oven exhaled Calor gas, and Calor gas surged up a vertical metal pipe leading to a lamp unit installed for illumination.

If I wished to leave the living-room after dark, I collected a candle in a quaint metal holder. Patches of candlelight and deep, deep shadows gave to the bothy a sense of mystery.

The living-room was heated by a coal fire (the coal supply was contained in a sack in an outbuilding roofed, in the West Highland way, with corrugated iron). A back-boiler was fitted. The draught was such that I thought the roar of the fire would be heard in the next glen. Upstairs, the cistern was of a size to provide water for three baths at a time.

It was a snug lodging. The living-room walls were lined with wood, keeping in the heat of the fire. This woodwork was unadorned by pictures or ornaments – until I hung a half-eaten cast antler I found on the hill. It was to the memory of the stalkers of old whose names cannot now be recalled.

Upstairs lay a bedroom, capacious landing (which became

my main food store) and bathroom. In the low upper rooms, I moved with my body shaped like a question mark. The dormer window tended to radiate cold from outside; it was like having a refrigerator with an open door. The beds were notable, their frames being of ornate ironwork; they were possibly quite valuable as antiques.

I took over the bothy with a sinking heart (the building was a little foisty, through infrequent use) but I left a week later with a lump in the throat – and not from the porridge!

At first, some 'fettling' was necessary. I found a clothes line strung across the back garden between large trees, but no clothes pegs could be seen. I fashioned some from old wire. No axe was provided, and so I chopped up wood for kindling using the edge of a roofing slate. Every session of wood-chopping was fraught with danger. I regularly took stock of my fingers.

The bothy was old enough for it to be accepted by wildlife round about. Each window offered fascinating views. A buzzard swept the hillside 200 yards away and pitched down on the very top of a holly tree, which for the next ten minutes resembled a totem pole. Tawny owls called from a large ash tree. I heard the familiar hooting and also the sharp *kewick* call of the female.

And, of course, there was the badger. I heard from a local family that it entered their yard to lick the fatty deposits from the end of the waste pipe leading from their kitchen. One evening, seeking to discourage the badger, they let out the dog. The badger was heard to growl. The dog whined for readmission to the house. Once, shining a powerful electric torch on to the back garden when the dustbin fell over, I saw the badger shuffling away on its short legs.

I was adopted by a cat. She was reputedly fifteen years old, and it seemed that nearly every cat in the glen was either her lover or offspring. What adventures had befallen her during those fifteen years I do not know – and foolishly, I did not inquire – but she was passing her old age pleasantly, commuting between her home and the bothy. The moment I peered from the doorway (or opened the upper part of the kitchen window) I saw a streak of black. The cat entered.

She purred so loudly, so long, that I wondered if hard purring could make a cat hoarse.

I saw her rubbing against a chair, back arched, tail up, forepaws kneading the carpet. Sometimes I allowed her to stay, and provided her with food. At other times – remembering the quantity of food lying about the bothy – I evicted her. She did not hold me a grudge. Her loud purring continued as I carried her through the rooms. The purring stopped at the very moment I put her on the ground in the cold, damp outdoors.

When I went to bed, the last task was to blow out the candle. On moonlit nights, I looked out of the window, and had my gaze returned by the black cat, which had settled down on the ledge outside.

The bothy is linked in my mind with attempts to cook typical Scottish fare. I prepared a couple of haggis (haggi?) purchased at a shop in Perth. They were excellent, but I developed thirst to an unbelievable degree. (Your Scotsman presumably has a bottle of whisky beside him). After tasting the contents of the first grey-brown, string-tied haggis, I had a desire to rush to the nearest burn and drain it.

The kitchen also handled half a dozen trout freshly caught in the lochan. These were native trout, not the introduced Loch Leven variety. Though rather small, the growth of the fish having been stunted by poor feeding conditions, they had a delicate flavour. The heads and tails were offered to the cat. The main part of the fish, gutted and cleaned and rolled in oatmeal, was fried.

My porridge was unfit for human consumption and would have been best used smoothing out some of the cracks around the kitchen sink. I bought loose oatmeal (there was no printed packet with instructions on how to prepare porridge). When I was not stirring the mixture I used my surplus energy to break up the lumps! In the autumns of years ago, the stalker's wife would have received winter stores, including quantities of oatmeal totalling some three hundredweight. She had in mind the long winter, and the possible blocking of the road by snow.

On chill autumn evenings, it was a delight to enter the bothy, and escape from the shadowy gloom of the glen. The building is in continuous shadow for nearly four months. It must be a pleasant lodging when the wind is sauching (roaring) and the tenant has had the delectable experience of lighting a fire in a cold room.

Here, within minutes of his return, he would also have a fifteen-year-old cat for company . . . .

12

Painted Loch

The hills that shelter Loch Hourn spring directly from the water's edge to heights around the magical 3,000 feet mark, above which devotees of Mr Munro excitedly romp. Ladhar Bheinn is one of the attractions. At 3,343 feet, it is the most westerly mainland Munro. Seen from the east, it offers a massive grey-blue rock wall with turrets – a lump of grand scenery that has been compared to that of the Dolomites.

On calm days, Loch Hourn reflects the hills in such detail that you are never quite sure where the water ends and the landscape begins. I have seen this stretch of water when the reflection has been tonally stronger than the actual features: when the picture has appeared to be inverted, like that to be seen through the ground-glass screen of an old plate camera.

The reflective qualities of Loch Hourn – based on its sheltered position between lofty hills – are confusing if daylight is fading and you happen to be at the tiller of a small boat with an hour of voyaging to complete before supper. This was my lot on a day when I spent far too much time on Ladhar Bheinn. I reached the boat at sundown. So deep were the reflections I had to take my bearings relative to a narrow strip of silver down the middle: the sky's contribution to a mosaic of form and colour. A voyage that began around Barrisdale Bay with the aura of pink afterglow ended by starlight!

On another day, Loch Hourn's surface was slightly ruffled. The picture formed on the water was crudely focused; it had dissolved into blotches of colour such as a painter of abstracts likes to apply to canvas. Brown blotches on the loch matched the areas of heather on the nearby hill. Copper blotches were out-of-register impressions of tracts of bracken, the fronds of which had become spectacularly bright as they went through their death agonies and collapsed. A smudge of gold on the water was a reflection of massed birches with tinted leaves. Grassland, now drained of sap, contributed areas of cream and fawn to the Painted Loch. The dark green originated from mountain pine or – in some cases – from holly.

One evening, the wake of the boat formed a herring-bone pattern on still water. The surface of Loch Hourn was banded blue-grey and pink, the former being a distorted image of distant hills, the latter the tone of the sky at sundown. On a day when a brisk wind raced in from the Sound of Sleat, and a strong tide was running, Loch Hourn was no longer 'painted'. Under cloud, all was reduced to gunmetal grey.

Gavin Maxwell knew the moods of this region, most particularly the area in which Loch Hourn opens out into the sound. His books, including the immortal *Ring of Bright Water,* were based on experiences at the fictitious Camusfearna ('bay of the alders'). Maxwell's otters frolicked along the beach and at the waterfalls of Lower Sandaig. Further east, Loch Hourn becomes narrow, secluded – as snug as a Norwegian fjord, with which it has often been compared.

I thought of Viking adventurers sailing into the loch, their longboats having central masts draped with vertically striped sails. Did they make the echoes ring with blasts produced by blowing into gargantuan horns? This is a district for echoes. When I shouted in a glen near Barrisdale, the echoes resounded and brought from a patch of shadow a sleepy-looking red deer hind.

Norse links are found everywhere. The names include Ar-nis*dale* and Barris*dale*. The people are thinly distributed, as in Norse times, when the typical man was uneasy in a crowd. The wife of an estate worker who was living in a glorious setting of hill, glen and loch winced when I mentioned several large Highland towns. She preferred life in this remote area, where it was possible to know everyone and where she could have a daily experience of the changing seasons.

I had not intended to visit Loch Hourn. Yet here I was, heading north-westwards from Fort William. I stopped at In-vergarry for petrol (it was my last chance to fill up the tank). I continued by Loch Garry and Loch Quoich (where I was told to pronounce the name 'coo-ick'). The road dipped between rocky hillsides, by a thundering burn and, with many a blind corner, ended – with the terminal emphasis of an exclamation mark – at the boat landing, Kinloch Hourn.

In truth, I craved for wilderness conditions after seeing the new bridge strung, Meccano-like, above the Leven narrows near Ballachulish. A modernistic road pattern lay between the bridge and village. I also felt cheated at Fort William. The main street is now bypassed. The old way had colour and excitement. The flanking shops offer almost everything Scottish, from haggis to full Highland dress.

I sped out of Fort William and passed some of the buildings of the Great Glen Cattle Ranch. An hour or so later, having left the main road to the Kyle, I was motoring between gentle hills on my way to what I think of as the Painted Loch.

Larch trees stood primly behind a deerproof fence. On three of the trees stood blackcock – a sight to remind me of a spring-time jaunt to these parts. I stopped in this very area to examine a patch of bog myrtle, a common enough plant in the west. It was mid-afternoon, in late April, and while enjoying the aromatic quality of the bog myrtle I heard a pigeon-like cooing, emanating from a point up the hillside.

The persistent sound was vibrant, and I identified it as the roo-cooing of a blackcock, a single bird. When I located it, I saw it puffed up like a turkey in its pride. The excited bird was jumping into the air from its perch on a grey boulder, around which was a tangle of dead bracken fronds, young conifers and straddling grasses.

Blackcock usually give voice when assembled at the *lek*, a display ground frequented at dawn and quite often in the after-noon. Several birds arrive to demonstrate their power and good looks at mating time. Never before had I seen a lone blackcock display in mid-afternoon.

I suspected that a female – known as the greyhen – was within a few yards of this bird, for he was out to impress. The drooped wings accentuated his size and bulk. His tail feathers were raised to show a gleaming white patch composed of the under-tail coverts. When the blackcock turned his head, a red wattle flashed in the sunlight. I watched a female clamber on to a rock and stay here for a few moments during which the cock bird became even more fervent. I did not see them mate.

In autumn, grouse fly the gauntlet of the guns. The powerful blackcock tends to zoom up higher than the red grouse and its downfall is sometimes a consequence of its great curiosity. It will circle, as though trying to locate the source of the disturbance which sent it winging from cover. A Highlander who regularly shot blackcock told me he was paid £2 for each tail he supplied to a famous Scottish regiment, now defunct. The tail was used to adorn bonnets.

At Tomdown, I stopped near a Victorian inn and looked across loch and hill to a blue distance. The inn was used by drovers of cattle, who gathered here to chat, to drink, to drink again. These men were using old routes from Knoydart and Glenelg that converged at Tomdown.

The waves on Loch Quoich were foam-crested. A considerable stretch of water tosses and frets behind man-made dams. Anglers know the water for its sporting fish, though a friend who went out to fish from a boat told me: "There was nothing moving that day except the boat and two bottles of whisky."

Outcropping rocks had become perches for cormorants. I looked in vain for the sight of a bird with outspread wings, a posture frequently adopted and beloved of nature photographers. A cormorant swam low in the water – its back was awash – and it stared at me with bright eye set in a head which had a strong reptilian appearance.

A heron flapped its powerful way just over the water. Herons find rich pickings in the cool, clear waters. (Later, by Loch Hourn, I would disturb a heron and see it flying high, close to a hillside, in the mist, where I would normally look for ravens.)

The hill burns support an astonishingly large population of trout. A friend caught six of them before he went through the formality of putting a lure on the hook; he fared even better after that! The fish were small, though some looked old. Their growth had been restricted by a scarcity of food. His best fish was about six inches in length, weighing somewhere between four and five ounces.

I motored by a lochan where, in spring, I had watched a red

stag emulating the moose. Before the hills green up, any source of protein is welcome and a stag will wade into the water and dip its head almost to the eyes to tug at young reeds, munching them appreciatively. Elsewhere, there are few fresh pickings until late in May. The snow, the wet and the cold weaken the deer to the extent that some of them "tip over". I quote a stalker.

Some red deer are fed on nutritious food pellets. Anxious to have quality stags, the owners of deer forests augment the rations. The stags put on more flesh and their antlers become heavier, more imposing. These 'feeders' stay near the road for months on end. I have seen them grazing even during the height of the day, when most self-respecting deer are laid up, awaiting twilight. In autumn, they are up the hill on the rutting grounds. In their upward journey, they pass the grisly remains of the old, the weak, the infirm, or those inexperienced young-sters who perished in the long season of food scarcity. The skeleton of one calf I found was lodged between boulders. Skeletal remains were held by a tangle of boulders in a burn. I presume that this body had been washed from high ground.

The mellow autumn sunshine, and a sparkle from lochan and burn, induced drowsiness. I lay on the hill, intending to soak up the warmth before going to shadowy Kinloch Hourn. Some local homes have no direct sunlight upon them from the end of October until February.

Several hours later I regretted having taken a siesta. The small of my back and my legs were colonized by ticks.

If, after a spring or autumn jaunt in the west, you feel an irritation on arm or leg, resist the temptation to scratch. It may be that you are host to a tick. A scratch removes the blood-bloated body of the animal but leaves the head in your body. A man who collected a tick on the sensitive skin between two fingers unwisely flicked the critter away. This happened four years ago. He still occasionally feels an itch from the infected place!

The tick that takes a ride on you is at first diminutive – a mere fleck of black. It begins to drink blood, and swells to the size of a pea. Its body is now dark, rotund. The classic method of re-moving a tick can be nasty in itself. Apply the tip of a lighted cigarette to the creature and, not surprisingly, it will withdraw its hold and fall off. I flicked off a tick body and was left looking at the dark blodge of the tick's head within the wound. So I was advised to scrub the area with water and carbolic soap to dislodge the head. The treatment was grimmer than the tick bite. I stroked a tick with a cigarette, and again I wish I had left it and allowed it to fall off naturally when its thirst was assuaged. The risk of using a cigarette is that you may suffer from third-degree burns!

A friend and I experimented with various substances and eventually found one that was effective and painless – whisky! The ticks died happily, and with a burp!

Western ticks attach themselves to the deer in such numbers that a stag from this region is readily identified by dealers in venison. A friend suggests that the presence of ticks, and their grim method of feeding, gave rise to the name 'red deer'. Dogs become hosts to ticks. I stroked the chin of a stalker's dog, and when I withdrew my hand the fingers were smeared with blood. This tick, neatly removed by the stalker, was at least three-eighths of an inch long. There was so much blood on the neck of the dog I had the impression its throat was cut.

My reverie on the hill did have a pleasant interlude. Long before ticks came into my life, I watched a golden eagle sweep over a hill-edge and traverse the district at a height of a few yards. Its huge shadow trailed the ground behind it as it rode, unflapping, on broad pinions. This eagle impressed me because it was, in effect, gliding *into* the wind.

The wings turned up gracefully at the tips. The primaries stood out individually, like dark fingers. The eagle was operating so low that whenever it reached an outcrop of rock I felt it must surely alight. It remained aloft, following the hillside to the ridge and going out of sight some twenty minutes after I had located it.

The golden eagle takes food at every opportunity. Sometimes it kills; at other times it settles on the body of a deer or sheep, stealing flesh as a vulture does. Several stalkers have mentioned to me seeing eagles that had become so sated with carrion they were, for a little while, incapable of flight.

Motoring on, I crossed the watershed. The countryside improved in appearance and interest. A whooper swan – a singleton – rode at anchor at the edge of a peat-brown expanse of water that was fringed with weed.

I decided to climb a hill, choosing Sgurr Dubh, partly because I knew of old a rough path that zigzags to the heights and offers reasonable gradients. As I climbed, I looked around on a countryside that offered classic examples of glaciation – of the grinding and plucking action of ice. Little bird life was present. I saw a meadow pipit and heard the bass-baritone voice of a raven. When I flushed four red deer near the summit they went clatteringly over the top.

I had lunch, my back resting on grey rocks. Not far away was a line of rusty uprights which, with some ancient wire once composed a fence where two marches met. Now it was possible to cross the fence at any point. I had selected a luncheon-place with a view, and what a view it was: of Loch Hourn, deep-sunk between knobbly hills in their autumn tints, with the odd patches of snow on sheltered highspots. Far to the west were the dreamy islands. I instantly recognized the Cuillins on Skye.

The sunlight strengthened, and Sgurr Dubh gleamed and glistened. Fragments of mica caught the light head on. A boulder was almost white in sunlight, being encrusted with crystals. Large pieces of mica gleamed with a mirror-like radiance, and it seemed that dozens of heliographs were flashing. When I removed a strip of mica and began to peel it, the pieces came away like leaves ripped from a book.

A pair of ravens gave voice as they glided above a gorge extending to the edge of Loch Hourn. Down by the water, a deltaic stretch of land had buildings upon it but no one was visible there.

I was enjoying food while sitting near the summit of Sgurr Dubh one day in April when a skein of wild geese passed over. I recalled on this latest visit the farmyardy calls, at first distant, then loud and clear as a chevron of greylags – fifty-eight individuals – swept low over the hill. The underparts were lit by the sun, revealing the fine-feather detail. The geese were moving north-westwards and when they were high over Loch Hourn a leadership change took place at the point of the chevron.

I continued to Kinloch Hourn. The road I followed made a steady descent but wound a good deal to account for the whims of local topography. I heard the rush of water in a burn deep-sunk and obscured by birch and pine. The wall between road and burn was topped off by grass, which hinted at the high rainfall in this western region of sea lochs and lofty hills.

When Kinloch Hourn came into view, I saw that everything human was on a small scale; it could not compete with the magnificence of the hills. A bridge across the burn was decked with wooden planks. The best land was bordered by deer-fencing. Across the valley lay the big house, with stands of fine timber on the hillside beyond.

Gulls wailed over marshland which twice a day is covered by tidal water. . .

13

To Hell — and Back!

In Gaelic mythology, Loch Hourn is a haunt of the Devil. The name is said to be derived from 'Iutharn', meaning Hell. I think of Kinloch Hourn as a heavenly place.

I was greeted by Highland ponies – over a dozen stocky, dependable ponies used for pony-trekking. One of their excursions extends across Scotland to the east coast and back, a matter of 200 miles. The Highland pony is compact and averages 14.2 hands high; a few individuals reach 15 h.h. The grazing area of this little drove extended well up the hills, where they had many opportunities to demonstrate their sureness of foot. In winter, their diet is augmented by imported provender.

Such a pony has been used for many years to carry the bodies of deer from the hills to the larder at the shooting lodge where the flesh is hung. A few ponies have to be blindfolded; most of them accept the load without fuss. I have heard of garrons – their name in the deer forest context – that would return untended to the larder down at the shooting lodge. They were loaded, given a pat on their haunches, and would set off along hill tracks they had known since their earliest days. The garron uses short steps to allow for the swing of the awkward load.

On one Highland deer forest, where no ponies are kept, the bodies of deer are transported on a stretcher-like frame supported by a single large wheel.

There is a spirit of remoteness at Kinloch Hourn. The road ends with a flourish by a stone jetty. The hills encircling the area have no conspicuous break, forming a delightful horseshoe shape. Remote Loch Hourn is best explored by boat. I launched a fourteen-footer which had an outboard engine – and hurriedly hauled out the craft when I realized it still contained a heavy

stone being used to hold down a tarpaulin and I had forgotten
to replace the plug. Ten minutes were spent in bailing out!

I saw wading birds scurry like grey mice at the edge of the
marsh, which was drying out with the tide's ebbing. Several
herons were present, and I began to think of Loch Hourn as
Loch Heron.

The water was gin-clear. I looked down to a bed littered with
shells and mysterious forests of weed. The weed swayed gently.
A tide which had come on without bluster was ebbing quietly,
imperceptibly. I saw no one.

Back in the eighteenth century, a quite large population was
assembled around Loch Hourn. Several hundred people lived
at Arnisdale alone. Work was provided by the cultivable
land and by the shoals of herring that entered the loch and
were netted from boats. In some years, the herring harvest
totalled 30,000 barrels.

Thomas Pennant visited Loch Hourn in its economic heyday;
he wrote in 1772:

> So unexpected a prospect as the busy haunt of men and ships in
> their wild and romantic tract afforded this agreeable reflection:
> that there is no part of our dominions so remote, so inhospitable,
> and so unprofitable as to deny employ and livelihood to thousands;
> and that there are no parts so polished, so improved, and so
> fertile, but which must stoop to receive advantage from the dreary
> spots they so affectedly despise; and must be obliged to ack-
> nowledge the mutual dependency of part on part, however remote-
> ly placed, and however different in modes and manner of living.

The shoals of fish vacated Loch Hourn. The people who
decided to remain here stoically attuned themselves to declining
prosperity. Some families clung to their traditional life through
the terrible days of potato blight; a number fell victim to
typhoid.

Evidence of former busy times was not hard to find. I saw
the line of a drovers' route on the southern side of the loch.
The position of this narrow track was indicated by retaining
walls constructed of dry stones (no mortar was used), with
many small gaps to allow for the passage of water draining from
the spongy hills behind. The drove road I contemplated came

from Knoydart. Another track, north of the loch, links up with Glenelg.

Loch Hourn was silent, colourful – a painted loch. I directed the boat towards a moderately large island, Eilean Mhogh-sgeir, which is craggy in parts and luxuriant with heather, blaeberry and small trees. Every footstep I took on the island revived memories of my last visit, in spring, when herons were nesting in trees at the eastern end and mallard sat on clutches of eggs under a screen of heather. Eider drakes jerked back their heads as they crooned to the females during the heady courtship days.

I neared the top of a ridge, coming under the bland gaze of a red stag which had cast its antlers. Only the stag's head and neck were in view, and it immediately turned – and vanished. I presume it swam across the fifty-yard channel to the mainland, a feat it could accomplish in a few minutes. A stalker whose dog put up a stag beside Loch Hourn watched that stag swim the whole width of the loch in quick time. I found copious deer droppings – and a matched pair of antlers!

My boat cruised on water so calm that the passing gulls could admire their reflections. Then I noticed that the northern shore had put out a long, low promontory as though to tickle the grey cliffs on the southern side. Thankfully it did not quite succeed in making contact. The narrow gap was my channel into the broader reaches of Loch Hourn, and I christened it the Jaws of Hell, which may or may not be original. In the Jaws, the tide plucked at the boat's rudder. No spray marked the turbulence, but I watched with fascination as the dark water whirled and bubbled, like soup coming up to the boil.

In spring, Loch Hourn is dotted with sea birds. The black guillemot bobs like a two-tone cork (black and white) far from those seaside cliffs where its cousin, the common guillemot, enjoys life in a crowd, jostling for space on narrow ledges. The black guillemot is never in a throng. Birds nervously dipped their heads into the water as I passed and they took on the semblance of butterflies when, taking flight, they showed off the white patches on their wings. One morning during springtime on Loch Hourn my boat overtook a solitary puffin.

Beyond the Jaws I found a landing place, drawing the boat up on to a beach composed of shells and rounded pebbles. I strode along a ridge to the grassy summit of Eilean Choinnich, where there is an old burial ground. The gravestones were rough; I could not find a single inscription. The stones, weathered over many years, were more than half-way towards becoming natural-looking outcrops. Oystercatchers enlivened the day with their calling. A curlew stalked on the wet mud.

So to Arnisdale. The loch was broader now; the hills less impressive because they no longer jostled for space at the very edge of the water. In Arnisdale Bay, seaweed was being taken to an ingenious floating machine that processed it for industrial use. I passed a rocky island which held an array of cormorants.

The homes of Arnisdale formed a one-street community around the bay, with Ben Sgritheall (3,196 feet) warding off the worst of the weather. Inquiring anxiously about retail outlets for cigarettes, I was told that none existed. When I returned to Arnisdale ten minutes after leaving it – to collect a rucksack I had left behind accidentally! – I was greeted by the man who had given me the bad news about cigarettes. He had a packet of twenty in his hand, which he sold to me!

An hour later I had beached the boat at the mouth of Loch Hourn. Before me was the Sound of Sleat and Skye. My companions on the water were two great black-backed gulls, and I watched a golden eagle glide over a ridge on the southern side of the loch. Here was a Crusoe-like solitude, and I even found human tracks on the beach.

The flow tide assisted my return to Kinloch Hourn. I might have been voyaging through Injun Country, though the watchers on the flanking hills were red deer, not Red Indians. No part of my voyage escaped from the scrutiny of a hundred unblinking eyes.

I turned the boat to starboard. Islets were being used as dormitories by common seals. Twenty animals stared, wriggled, splashed and sped away, leaving exploding bubbles of air and swirling water to mark their passage.

On the first autumn voyage, I knew that I would have to climb the sombre crags of Ladhar Bheinn. A whole day was devoted to the ascent. I directed the boat to the now-familiar white beach at the mouth of Barrisdale Bay. During my walk around Barrisdale to the starting point for Ladhar Bheinn, I chatted with the wife of an estate worker who told me that her children were at school at Inverness. Prior to this, they had attended school at Glenelg, making a twice-daily crossing of the loch to Arnisdale and being conveyed on to Glenelg by the school bus.

Does the Beast of Barrisdale still wander in this area? The Beast has three legs (two legs fore, one aft) and is reputed to have its den in the Knoydart Hills. No one has reported seeing it since 1880. The only figure I saw on my climb was a middle-aged man who, while descending, decided it was too hot for clothes, which he promptly removed. He was now clad in binoculars and boots!

I followed a zigzag way up the foothills as a silver monoplane circled the dale and landed in a field beside the shooting lodge. So still was the air, and so clear the water of Loch Hourn, that Barrisdale Bay seemed to have a leaf pattern, the shallows appearing as expanses of green and the deeper channels fine veins of blue. I lost a little height, rounded a corner – and found myself in what could have been the Dolomites.

In the foreground, the land sloped to where a burn ran in foamy spate. The glen beyond was moderately broad. It led to a formidable rock wall, most of it grey-blue from shadow, though sunlight banded it and emphasized the dominantly vertical form. Several peaks stood up from the wall like the turrets of a medieval castle. Some of the gullies between the peaks held patches of snow.

In the glen, the air was languid. I found some solace from the heat by bathing my face in the burn. Then I settled down for lunch, with entertainment provided by yet another golden eagle. It went through a routine similar in many ways to that seen near Loch Quoich – gliding low down and eventually winging up to the ridge. This eagle collected power from a thermal and allowed itself to be carried high. In minutes, it was merely a speck against the blue.

My map showed a feature called 'bealach' (which usually means a pass); it was the obvious way to the skyline. How wrong I was in selecting it. My surplus energy was used up in withdrawing my feet from the boggy land into which they sank for several inches at every footfall. I negotiated a collection of assorted stones and boulders and found myself looking at a slope like a house side.

During one of several resting periods, I watched a red stag running with hinds. Low in the glen were peaty areas where the stag had wallowed in a porridge-like mixture from which it had emerged dark and glistening. The most interesting plants I found were stagshorn (a commoner) and expanses of woodrush.

The glen was quiet – strangely quiet to one from the Pennines where it is not possible to walk a yard without hearing a sheep bleating. In spring, the crags of Ladhar Bheinn echo to the fluty songs of cock ring ouzels.

After the bogs and the bealach (Gaelic with Groans!), I reached the skyline. Now surely I would have the pleasure of a ridge walk. Instead of country suited to a jog-trot I found the assorted hilltops were quite substantial and gorges lay between them. The summit of the main peak seemed to retreat from me as I slogged over turf and boulders. At least, Ladhar Bheinn was clear of the mist and cloud which drape it on most days of the year. And I could continue to watch deer through binoculars. The animals were specks of reddish-brown against the tussocky grasses.

The highest point was attained after a number of 'false summits'. I looked down on hill ranges that were beginning to take on the pinkish hue of a sky in which the sun was dipping. A grassy ridge led me to a triangulation point, on which some-one had left a slab of Windermere butter fudge. I bombarded the fudge with snowballs.

It is only human to believe that once you have reached the highest point all the climbing is over for the day. On the way back to Barrisdale, I had to lose height, but then I trudged upwards to negotiate the top of Stob a' Choire Odhair. I left the ridge, and tussocky slopes led me into the glen. There seemed to be miles of gruelling descent, in which every tussock threatened to twist an ankle and incapacitate me. I slipped into three boggy areas. By the time the burnside was reached, I had enough wet peat on me to be taken for a stag at rutting time!

I stopped twice to rest my ankles, and once when I had an unexpectedly good view of a stag herding hinds. One of the hinds saw me, of course. The deer trotted off down the slope.

The zigzag path into Barrisdale was my salvation. Here, as I bounced along, I recovered some of my strength and spirits. When I regained the flatlands, a three-mile walk to the boat was tolerable. Here, joined by a friend, I experienced an hour's voyage that began in the gloaming and ended at the edge of darkest dark, with the stars offering a faint, cold light for the final approach.

I do not recommend a nocturnal voyage in a small boat. The tide plucked at the rudder when I was negotiating the Jaws of Hell. Elsewhere, so calm was Loch Hourn, and so deep the reflections, that we could not establish the precise line of the shore. We crossed a stretch of loch where, next day, a cormorant was seen apparently perched on water. It was found to be occupying a substantial rock that only just broke surface!

On another outing in this district of hill and painted water, I leapt from boulder to boulder along the bed of one of many burns plunging towards Loch Hourn. My world shrank to a narrow, rocky channel down which the sterile water creamed and bubbled. Stones that had fallen into the round holes eroded by the burn were now, themselves, being made round as marbles by the constant swirling action of the water. Here and there, the burn had laid down for itself natural chutes from which water poured as a clear and even flow. I could actually look through the top of a waterfall and beyond, for many yards, into the clear, green-tinged world of the burn. Stones of many hues, brought down from the heights, nudged into rounded shapes, lay like jewels in a submerged vault.

I entered a wide, grassy area where the burn's roar became little more than a murmur. Birches grew from crevices in boulders. Another line of lusty poles and some taut wire marked yet another territorial division.

When the visit was over, the magic of Loch Hourn endured until, once again, I had crossed the watershed and was heading, a little regretfully, for the Great Glen. I do not decry the district beyond. It has a beauty of its own. But Loch Hourn and its environs are magnificent. A buzzard perched on a pole near the road was the last bird I saw before entering what I now like to think of as the outer world.

Henceforth, every mile of the way seemed to be in countryside a shade more civilized than that I had left. At Tomdown, ploughs were ripping up ground leading down to the loch, preparing for the planting of yet another crop of conifers. Loch Garry seemed devoid of bird life. In spring, the cigar-like form of a black-throated diver had been seen.

I joined the much-improved Road to the Kyles, then the Great Glen. Spean Bridge provided me with food and the car with petrol. I was hustled through Fort William at unseemly haste by the new road. The new bridge over Loch Leven spared me twenty miles of travel round the loch or a wait for space on one of the little ferryboats that, for years before the bridge was made, operated a shuttle-service across the turbulent narrows.

There were now many modernistic touches to the landscape. My mind refused to relinquish memories of unspoilt Loch Hourn – of its brilliant reflections; of the Jaws of Hell and its guardian herons and cormorants; of the long, languid view from Ladhar Bheinn over a landscape where, as yet, man seems to have left few marks.

14

Great Glen

Macaulay claimed, on little or no evidence, that Glencoe means The Glen of Weeping. Was he thinking about the 1692 massacre, which colours every consideration of Scotland's best-known glen? Or was it a comment on the rainfall – some 90 inches a year?

Glencoe is, to me, a glen of surprises. I had seen it at Easter, when the weather forecasters dolefully prophesied up to nine inches of snow in northern Scotland. A short-lived blizzard whitened my home district on the evening before I ventured north. Next morning no trace of snow was visible, and the sky had run out of cloud.

The prospect of encountering nine inches of snow in the Highlands faintly troubled me, but in the event Rannoch Moor looked benign. The great peaks around Glencoe were silvery with snow and mist, but the glen itself appeared to smoulder, such was the effect of bright light on the dun colours. I trudged for half a mile before my eyes were seared by a desert of snow crystals.

Visiting Glencoe in June, I prepared for rain. It always rains during a Highland summer! But the hills were baked hard, and their vegetation scorched, by unrelenting sunshine and high temperatures. It was the first time I had walked in and around Glencoe without getting my feet wet.

Now, in autumn, I reached Glencoe during a period of bright weather to find that, for one day, cloud had drawn a curtain across the sun. The light was flat. Mist blunted the edges of the crags.

Nonetheless, around me was what a seventeenth-century writer called the "wyld rockish country of Glencoe". I followed the Devil's Staircase towards Kinlochleven – a route favoured by some of the old-time drovers of cattle. The roaring sound I heard was not made by beef cattle; several unseen stags were responding to the high feelings of the rut by giving voice.

Up there, on the misty hills, these words written by Sir Walter Scott seemed especially appropriate. They were plucked from *The Massacre of Glencoe:*

> Say, harp'st thou to the mists that fly,
> Or to the dun deer glancing by,
> Or to the eagle that from high
>   Screams chorus to thy minstrelsy? —
> No, not to these, for they have rest, —
> The mist-wreath has the mountain-crest,
> The stag his lair, the erne her nest,
>   Abode of lone security.
> But those for whom I pour the lay,
> Not wildwood deep, nor mountain gray,
> Not this deep dell, that shrouds from day,
>   Could screen for treach-rous cruelty.

Romance had entered my soul, though I had resolved before entering this Great Glen not to brood upon the details of the infamous massacre nor to ponder with dewy eyes on this sublime landscape. Which, indeed, is the most nightmarish event in Scottish history? My own selection is the massacre of the inhabitants of the island of Eigg, not by sword, but by smoke. A rival clan found they had taken sanctuary in a cave on the southern coastline, and they lit a fire at the narrow entrance and suffocated them. When I last visited the cave, a child's doll had been lodged between stones high on the entrance arch. My heart bled at the thought of the asphyxiated victims. I shudder at the thought of their misery. The Glencoe massacre, which colours every visitor's view of this tight little valley, affects me less deeply than does the grim story from Eigg.

Some books for climbers have reduced the features of Glencoe to simple codified statements. I was bored by the neatly tabulated facts and figures. It was enough to know that Glencoe is about eight miles long and extends from east to west; that the landmass includes Argyll's highest hill, Bidean nam Bian, which strokes the grey clouds at 3,766 feet. A

Yorkshireman who visited Glencoe described it as "nowt but scenery".

The scenery *is* dramatic, but first impressions – which tend to be the most enduring – will depend on the end from which you approach the glen. See Glencoe from the east, after crossing Rannoch Moor, and it is austere, rocky. The road bends, twists, is confined, runs near thundering water, escapes from constrictions and then sweeps downwards, passing the quiet loch of Triochatan, which offers a friendly gleam when all around is dark. The loch also reflects features of the hillsides. These are not bare, as you might suppose, but support many native trees.

Approach Glencoe from the west, and the main impression is of space and fertility. The rocks are plastered with alluvial deposits. Hillsides are now thickly planted with trees – various North American species, hinting at what it must be like in the Canadian Backwoods.

Mary Donaldson, a traveller in quite recent times, approached Glencoe from the west and considered that Loch Triochatan (once famous for its water bull) was the point at which the valley entered its second phase, "in which it shows a beauty grim and terrible. For the first part is a gradual climbing up through a fine wooded road ... From the loch onwards, however, the bleak and rugged mountains of the wild and narrow glen close in upon you increasingly and deeper and deeper grows the bed of the Coe until it becomes a veritable gorge through which the river plunges".

In Romantic times, writers were prepared to be overawed by the hills, on which they did not actually walk. A man called Leyden, however, did not mind climbing, and in 1800 he actually struggled up the hills. Of Coire nam Beith he wrote: "We discovered a vast chasm which, during our approach, the projections of the rock had concealed. The light cloud of mist resting upon these projecting sides formed a stupendous vault of airy aspect, beneath which we could distinctly perceive the steep side of a more distant and more elevated mountain spire rising in awful grandeur."

Leyden climbed further, passing tumbling water, to a place where "the water shoots over a precipice about 50 feet perpendicular". Beyond lay more rock grandeur:

> I was alone, elevated at a vast height in a sublime mountain recess; immense piles of rock as regular as ruins surrounded me on every side except where I ascended; the winds of the mountains descended in hollow gusts, and a dull-sounding stream murmured sullenly by.
>
> Over my head, the white cloud of mist formed a vast magnificent ceiling; some red deer appeared on the rocks above; and all around me lay strewn the blasted and withering birches of former times that had fallen and were falling of extreme old age to the ground.

Charles Dickens, his eye forever on the popular market, described the pass in 1841 in non-specific terms. He found himself in an "awful place". Many glens higher up "form such haunts as you might imagine yourself wandering in the very height and madness of a fever. They will live in my dreams for years – I was going to say as long as I live, and I seriously think so. The very recollection of them makes me shudder". Pause now for a yawn!

Genteel Victorians, snug in their over-furnished, over-heated drawing-rooms, viewed the world from behind lace curtains and potted aspidistras. They relied on the writers and artists to give them pictures of wilderness Britain. Paintings of the time show Glencoe rendered sombrely in oils, with swirling mist and glinting water.

Sometimes, cattle were portrayed. Dr John Stuart of Luss was reported in 1777 as stating that sea pink was among the richest and best kinds of herbage available to the black cattle "among the mountains of Glencoe". At the beginning of summer, the people of this glen drove their cattle to the lands in the east. Young folk and women lived a shieling life until autumn returned with a flurry of tinted leaves. The cattle were then driven back to the main settlements, some to be over-wintered, others to be slain and the flesh salted down for use in the winter, the surplus stock to be sold to southern graziers.

Came the sheep. Local people then looked back nostalgically to the old days. A visitor of 1818 observed that sheep-farming had done the work of extirpation – then a favourite, over-used word – "more effectively than the Secretary's massacre; but slight traces now remain of the warlike tribe in this little valley".

The Period before the Sheep cannot have been a bad time for Glencoe. A man could provide his family with the various products of cattle and sheep; he could grow some cereals and lift a few fish from Loch Leven. When the Wordsworths came to Glencoe, old people told Dorothy of the rosy yesteryears when Glencoe was noted for its corn production. She saw much poor land that was being used as pasturage for cattle; she also saw, and admired the hills, being (untypically) lost for phrases of her own devising, resorting to some by Milton, who had written that "his stature reacht the skie".

The horse that drew their wagon was again creating problems for the Wordsworths. At the approach to Glencoe it shied on seeing what turned out to be the shafts of an agricultural roller; these shafts protruded above a wall. When the horse reared in alarm, it damaged the harness and also the vehicle. Both were repaired, but they travelled into Glencoe with William riding the horse and Dorothy occupying a seat on the repaired cart, which was being driven by a helpful Highlander; he had loaned them his horse.

I saw pastoral or forested countryside gradually give way to the grander stuff, as volcanic rocks were revealed in dramatic upsweeps. Glencoe's remaining natural charms will be preserved, for about 12,000 acres are owned by the National Trust for Scotland.

The Forestry Commission has held thousands of acres in Glencoe and Glenachulish since the 1920s, and at the time of my visit a third of this acreage was reported to have been planted. I followed two of the forest trails. One – named Signal Rock trail, after the supposed signalling place used at the start of the massacre – included Ghrianain (Mound of the Sun), which is owned by the National Trust. Lochan Nature Trail, of about two miles was approached from Carnoch, alias Glencoe village. The lochan is artificial in the sense it was created when man flooded a peaty area. Lord Strathcona was the landowner who thus changed the local topography. Not only did he flood an area where for many years peat had been gathered as fuel but he built a fine house on what had been common grazing land.

Booklets issued for natural trails (all nature trails) tend to over-excite and then disappoint the visitor. He reads of exotic creatures like red and roe deer, wild cat, otter and mink, in the case of Glencoe, but the average visitor, following the track by day, returns with some notes about the chaffinch or the odd buzzard. In the early afternoon, all self-respecting mammals (apart from man) are lying up in cover.

The status of the road through Glencoe has been elevated to something approaching a motorway. Parking beside it, I felt the car creaking on its springs whenever a heavy lorry passed with a whine and a whoosh of displaced air. The previous road reconstruction was made in the early 1930s. The way was still quite rough and little used just after the 1939-45 war when some cyclist friends, on their way from Land's End to John o'Groats, reached Glencoe in the late afternoon. They remember the glen for its stillness and apparent absence of life. They told me: "We didn't see a soul between Tyndrum and Ballachulish."

A buzzard alighted on the parapet of a bridge; we eyed each other at a range of little more than twelve feet. The bird crossed over the road in a smooth gliding action, and actually had to ascend to attain the top of a fencing post on the other side.

My car shook as a another lorry passed. I remember the high pitch of noise, the displacement of air, a cloud of dust and, when the turbulence was over, had further sight of the buzzard. It had moved to the next post but one!

Glencoe had its many signs of modernity, including a wind-sock in a field (the device erected to assist the pilots of helicopters landing during rescue operations) and a metal bridge spanning a vinegar-brown river.

Further up the glen, I joined some visitors at The Study, or Queen's View, which is locally Innean a' Cheathaich, 'the anvil of the mist'. I believe the name 'study' was derived from 'stiddie', a form of anvil. Around us was the wilder Glencoe, with the bastions of lofty hills of such character that they might have been roughly hacked out by a sculptor rather than by the random forces of nature.

October is a good month in which to visit Glencoe. The air is calm, invariably dry. Gone from the deep glen are the tedious summer greens. Heavy snowfalls are reported to come after Christmas, and snow can remain on these magnificent hills until April or May.

The Glencoe preferred by discriminating visitors lies above 2,500 feet. On the high rock areas live ptarmigan; other bird life is relatively sparse, but the dotterel and snow bunting are said to have nested here.

I left Glencoe by the upper stretch that was hemmed in by dark rocks and ran close to where waterfalls were like prophets crying out in the wilderness.

For a time, the road has an air of mystery. Suddenly, it bursts free of constrictions. Into view come the broad sweep of Rannoch Moor, also Kingshouse, white-walled and looking diminutive in its setting at the head of Glencoe, a little way from the modern road.

In the eighteenth century, this hostelry had a poor reputation among travellers. Thomas Newte wrote that there was "not a bed in it for a decent person to sleep in, nor any provisions but what are absolutely necessary for the family". Southey, friend of the Wordsworths, who visited the place in the autumn of 1819, heard that the man who took over Kingshouse Inn ten years before had a capital of only £70. Yet he made enough in ten years for him to buy a large farm and to stock it with animals worth £1,500.

By implication, his customers at the inn had suffered . . . .

15

The Black Country

So many features on the wild moors east of Glencoe had been named 'Black' that I began to suspect there must have been a clan of that name in the area. I travelled near Blackrock Cottage, taking my eyes off the road for the few seconds necessary to fix in my mind a picture of Meall a' Bhuiridh with its chairlift, the first of its type to be erected in Britain.

I eased the car into a layby and studied the map, locating Black Corries (where, some years ago, a friend saw a white hind!), Black Water, and also 'Black' rendered in Gaelic and bestowed on many lesser features. My eyes ranged over Rannoch Moor and the Black Mount.

In this Scottish Black Country I looked hard for an object that was truly black, the 'colour' whose use is forbidden by art teachers. The plump body of a blackcock looked black. The peat under shadow was unattractively dark; then a cloud moved away, letting in the sunshine, and it became chocolate-brown.

Distant parts of Rannoch Moor were misty; my eyes moved restlessly for focal points at the western edge of these 20 square miles of squelchy terrain. The wet nature of Rannoch Moor was revealed soon after I left the road. I felt to be walking on a sponge. Water spurted at every footfall. The vapour, restless and chilly, brought to mind the coven of witches encountered by Macbeth.

When a gale frolics across these empty miles, it can knock the wind out of you. A few surviving pines wheeze like asthmatics, and any car emerging from Glencoe moves uneasily on its springs.

Rannoch is a basin of granite lying at around 1,000 feet above sea level. Liberally overlaid with peat, it holds water like a sponge because the drainage is impeded. The builders of the West Highland Railway found the peat was up to 20 feet deep in places.

Rannoch Moor is high-lying but much higher ground surrounds this old rock basin. Three-thousand-footers stand round about. The eye readily takes in their blocky forms, from Ben Lawers to Ben Cruachan, and including that most distinctive of outlines, the triangle of Schiehallion.

Visitors from England tended to judge landscape by the prettiness that surrounded them when they were at home in some cosy south country town or village. When prettiness was not the keynote of the scene, they tended to write in exaggerated fashion about the local rigours. An Englishman coming to Rannoch in 1792 thought the area was "not the mere negation of beauty, but the most positive and curious ugliness".

He looked at Buchaille Etive Mór, at the eastern approaches to Glencoe, and was not impressed, thinking of this formidable hill as being stripped of its natural covering by "some outrageous storm . . . the carcass of a mountain, peeled, sore and hideously disgustful".

Rannoch, though wild, tangled and squelchy, is undeniably romantic, a prime setting for mystery, intrigue, adventure, or all three. Stevenson knew it well. He wrote in *Kidnapped:*

> The mist rose and died away, and showed us that country lying as waste as the sea; only the moorfowl and the peewees crying upon it, and far over to the east a herd of deer, moving like dots. Much of it was red with heather; much of the rest broken up with bogs and hags and peaty pools; some had been burnt black in a heath fire; and in another place there was quite a forest of dead firs, standing like skeletons. A wearier-looking desert man never saw.

Rannoch has been fettered, if not actually tamed, by the works of man. Both road and rail cross over it. An old road went west of Loch Tulla and crossed the Black Mount to Blackrock Cottage and Glencoe. This road lost its importance in the 1930s, when the present A82 was made, extending between Bridge of Orchy and Glencoe and going east of Loch Tulla. The railway, over to the east, was set on the quivering bogs only after thousands of tons of material had been tipped along the line it was to take.

Today, a traveller on the A82 takes the rapid crossing of Rannoch Moor for granted; it unfolds as long, straight stretches. The driver, his foot hard on the accelerator, sees the Rannoch landscape as a tawny blurr as the miles rush by.

Two centuries ago, a pedestrian from Kingshouse, following the roughest of tracks, held his cloak tightly about him and muttered prayers for deliverance from the moor's perils, known and unknown. He made good progress if he maintained a rate of a mile an hour. John Knox, a traveller in the eighteenth century, said: "It is hardly agreed upon by travellers which is the line of road, everyone making one for himself. Even sheep follow better routes, understanding levels better and selecting better gradients."

It was mainly for the benefit of cattle-drovers that the master road-builder, Telford, planned an improved route, by Lochs Ossian and Lydoch to Killin, cutting out some fifteen miles of travel. Telford asked a friend to survey the route, and that was that. Even Telford must have shuddered at the thought of laying a hard road across an area where mats of sphagnum moss glow a brilliant green on many dull days.

Stevenson, in his prose picture of Rannoch, mentioned a few members of the local fauna. 'Moorfowl' was the old name for red grouse. 'Peewee' describes the springtime call of the cock lapwing. Stevenson included deer; these are noble red deer about which modern travellers are warned by roadside signs. The deer can be seen lying quite close to the road. At night, the headlamps of a car bring a response from their eyes. A row of leafless shrubs on the crest of the ridge may be the antlers of a recumbent group of stags.

In winter, Rannoch Moor may appear lifeless, but life exists if you look for it – even if the only evidence is a crow calling through a succession of solitudes. The moor is activated in spring by the return of wading birds to nest.

The curlew – 'whaup' of Old Scotland – glides with arched wings and opens its down-curved mandibles to utter a liquid song. The drier hillocks welcome a few golden plover, and these birds punctuate the lengthening days with their rather sad whistling. The black-and-gold of a plover's mantle tone with the vegetation, which has yet to freshen up. Snipe, flushed from boggy areas, give sneezes of alarm as they zigzag across the grey sky to safe distances.

One spring day I watched a cock merlin fly down a meadow

pipit. The merlin was only about the size of a mistle thrush but was, nevertheless, a fierce falcon. Having singled out a bird as prey, it hunted it with a relentless vigour that took into account every jink and side-slip of the victim.

Once – and once only – did I see a peregrine, in silhouette, flash across the sky. The wings, which were angled back, looked like scimitar blades. I have yet to see a golden eagle in this area. One pair about which I heard nested on a steep crag in remoter Rannoch. The crag face looked formidable, but he who walked around it found he could reach its head on gently rising ground. Then it was possible to peer directly into the eyrie.

An osprey pair nested on a tree jutting from an island in one of Rannoch's innumerable lochans. The fish-hawks were exterminated, but birds emanating from Scandinavian stock have recolonized the Highlands. It may soon be possible to see an osprey fishing at lochans where, today, the red-throated diver claims ownership.

A good friend heard of a white deer, a hind, in a remote part of Rannoch Moor. To find it became an obsession. He trudged for miles and questioned the local people. The hind was seen grazing near a loch, and in due course my friend saw it close enough for him to establish that its eyes were pink – it was a true albino. It was said that if anyone shot a white hind he would be visited by ill-luck.

Scrope – whom I will properly introduce later – heard of a white hind that appeared on the hills above Loch Etive, beyond the Black Mount. The superstitions believed that if another white hind was seen in the district it would presage death by violence. Early last century, both circumstances occurred. Scrope did not establish the precise date, but his "few years ago" would be about 1840. That winter, when the keepers were indoors because the hills were treacherous, crusted with snow and ice, poachers spread out to drive and kill red deer. Some men concealed themselves beside a small pass used by deer. Others went ahead to flush out the herd and drive it towards their hidden colleagues. Signals were used to report progress.

In the late afternoon, when the light was fading, one of the drivers brought his head above the skyline and held up his arms to indicate that the deer were in the pass below. The nearest marksman, looking into the murk, believed he was seeing the head and antlers of a stag. He fired. The approaching friend died from a gunshot wound in the head.

Because the men were acting illegally, the story did not become common knowledge. The body of the dead man was tossed over the rocks, becoming mangled; the other men then carried the remains to his home, and their account of a simple accident was accepted. The dead man's sister, laying out the body, found the gunshot wound, but the affair was hushed up.

Highland deer forest owners tended to cherish any associations with white hinds – true albinoes, creamy in the coat, with pink eyes. One such forest was the Black Mount, where – according to an old book kept at Taymouth – a white hind was seen in 1622. Reports of the unusual deer reached the King, and he sent three Englishmen to investigate.

A white hind was subjected to exaggerated tale-telling. Scrope was sceptical about claims of a long-lived animal of this type that was associated with Lochtreig. It was said to have been known to Captain Macdonald of Tulloch, in Lochaber, for fifty years. The captain died in 1776, aged eighty-six. "His father knew her an equal length of time before him, and his grandfather knew her for sixty years of his own time; and she preceded his days; these three gentlemen were all keen deer-stalkers." And, possibly, topers.

Just over 3,700 acres of Rannoch fall within a national nature reserve. Plants that do not mind getting their roots wet enliven the moorland year. There is bog asphodel, with its golden spikes, and sundew, finely glistening in sunlight. I collected a sprig of bog myrtle; it sweetly flavoured the boot of my car.

Trees are few in number. I saw some Scots pines, also a few gale-battered conifers in an experimental patch. The Words-worths saw neither tree nor shrub for miles but found where the peat had eroded was "a long decayed forest" now evidenced by "pieces of black mouldering wood". These were the famous bog trees. I saw lots of them in the ditches beside the modern road. Trees which grew many centuries ago were overwhelmed in a period of extreme wetness by the growth of peat.

Dorothy Wordsworth climbed a hill and saw her first wild, natural "Scotch firs". A thin sprinkling of these pines was visible; they were "thinned of their numbers, and left, comparatively, to a helpless struggle with the elements" but they impressed by their very gloom, even grandeur. William Macgillivray described the Scots pine in a book published in 1855 as "a gloomy and stubborn tree". (He preferred the birch, which "responds in its graces to the gentler emotions".) Magnificent stands of Scots pines occupied a hillside beside which I drove in Glen Orchy. On the other side of the river stood the modern spruce plantations.

The Black Mount, which lies south-west of Rannoch Moor, was known as Corrichibah or Coireach Ba. It surely took its name from peat, which is here exposed like slabby pieces of chocolate cake. You will know that a Highland forest may be totally devoid of trees; it is land set apart for the chase.

The Black Mount has been a forest since about 1600. I have already related that the interest of James IV was aroused in this hump of land when news reached him that a white hind had been seen here. Did his emissaries succeed in finding it? Were they completely successful in their mission, which was to convey the deer to one of the King's English parks?

In the history of the forest there have been periods when the native red deer have had to compete with sheep. The sheep were despatched in 1820, when the forest had been rented by Lord Breadalbane. Without competition at the grazings, the deer put on size and improved in quality; the numbers rose until it was estimated in 1839 that over 1,500 were present. They had a range of over 35,000 acres.

Black Mount stags were special. Scrope wrote: "The stags ... in 1839 exceed those of most of the neighbouring forests in point of weight, and may be estimated at an average of from 16 to 17 stones, imperial, sinking the offal; and they are frequently found to weigh eighteen, nineteen and even twenty-one stones, having two to three inches of fat on the haunches."

The Black Mount, added Scrope, was "peculiarly adapted for deer, being rocky and steep, and the hills are varied with numerous corries". Good wintering conditions were available on low ground, which produced very early grass in spring.

Then, said Scrope, "the deer might be seen standing in the water picking rushes and grass which grew at the sides of the river and lochs". He was referring to the "Bah Lochs". The deer were fond of going to the several wooded islands.

The Black Mount was sanctified by the presence of that most fashionable painter, Edwin Landseer. He was shown a high pass between corries through which deer went when being driven. Landseer sketched the area and worked up his impressions into a large canvas, adding deer and calling his painting 'The Deer Drive'. In 1912, when the acreage was about 90,000, during one hot spell of weather the 'cool mosses' of the Black Mount attracted between 2,000 and 3,000 deer.

On a dull day, I approached Rannoch Moor from the east, by Loch Tummel and Loch Rannoch – the early stages of the Road to the Isles. I drove right up to Rannoch station, which stands on a stretch of line the builders of the railway left until the last; for it raised the most difficult engineering problems.

The West Highland line benefited from the experience of George Stephenson, 'father' of railways, who found a novel way of 'floating' the tracks across Chat Moss, in Lancashire. 'Floating' is not a strictly accurate way to describe the application of faggots and other coarse substances to stabilize a bog.

When the railway engineers came to Rannoch, the only tracks they found were made by sheep. The line was opened in 1894, and a writer in a railway periodical observed that the line "throws open to the public wide and interesting tracts of country which have been almost as much unknown to the ordinary tourist hitherto as Central Africa was ten years ago to the geographer".

The weather was quite good for Rannoch. "Nobody could have wished a better day, except those who were anxious to see every clearly cut peak outlined against the sky – and then they would have paid the penalty of sweltering in the sunshine. The clouds swathed the mountaintops, but they did not dissolve into more than a few drops of rain."

The railway was used to transport the carcasses of deer from local estates. A special chute at Rannoch station assisted during the loading of the vans.

I quit Rannoch as a train consisting of diesel locomotive and wagons of timber moved across the landscape, dwarfed by the scale of the hills until it was something like a model. The train was delivering another load of Highland timber to the big pulp mills at Fort William.

16

Game Birds by Rannoch

Autumn is for grouse – red grouse, the stubby-winged moor-fowl. A crackle of gunfire at the moor-edge marks the beginning, in August, of a grouse-shooting season that extends into the season of "mists and mellow fruitfulness".

Coveys of plump grouse pass over the lines of butts with a whirring flight that alternates with gliding on stiff, down-curved wings. Seeing them producing bursts of power reminds me of the retired Glasgow tram driver who, when driving his car, scared the passengers by building up speed then slipping the gear lever into neutral and waggling it idly until, the speed of the vehicle declining, he neatly notched it into the appropriate gear and built up the speed again!

The grouse that survive make off low, hugging the contours, pitching among the heather to crow: *kowa, kowa.* The voice of a cock grouse has a strangely human quality and has been translated by the fanciful into "go back, go back".

The red grouse is a true Scot, with *scoticus* in its scientific name and such a regard for its native ground that it stays here, come wind, rain or blizzard, the whole year through. Weather conditions are extreme if it migrates to country lower than the moors on which it hatched out. If it can expose a little heather, and dig down to a place where some grit may be found, the red grouse can survive a blanket of snow. Grit is taken into the crop to help with the breakdown of the tough food.

Each autumn, grouse settle many a boundary dispute. A stretch of moorland has a certain carrying capacity that varies from year to year. It depends on the number of birds and the condition of *Calluna,* the basic food. Scientists based at Aberdeen University discovered that in autumn, when cocks stake their territorial claims, the strongest birds hold the territories and the surplus birds either find new ground or die off.

128

This is a considerable simplification of some protracted and involved research. Research work at Aberdeen has changed many of our basic ideas about red grouse. For instance, the old-style gamekeeper who spends so much of his time in a war against 'vermin' would be more usefully employed managing the moorland itself.

A glance at some of the old estate books is enough to indicate that the red grouse population tends to fluctuate in natural cycles. Before the Victorian obsession with vermin-destruction, grouse were perhaps wilder and possibly fitter than they are today.

The Victorians had the knack of building up the red grouse population to a level far above that decreed by nature. It was on Blubberhouses Moor, in Yorkshire, that Lord Walsingham blasted his way into the record books. On 28 August 1872, taking up breech-loaders and muzzle-loaders, he bagged 842 birds in twelve hours of shooting. Twenty drivers were employed, in two parties of ten each, and the number of drives was sixteen.

Then, on 30 August 1888, as though dissatisfied with the earlier demonstration of his prowess, Lord Walsingham shot at grouse for 14 hours 18 minutes. He fired a total of 1,550 cartridges and 1,070 birds were slain. It was said that he was responding to a bet made in a London club, and he employed two men to load his four breech-loaders. He brought down three grouse with a single shot.

High figures were also being recorded on the best grouse land in Scotland – that land towards the east which is drier than western areas. Today the sportsmen are less fervent than were their predecessors on the hill. They do not give the impression they want to blast the whole grouse stock into oblivion. They bag some grouse, a few ptarmigan, the odd woodcock and one or two mountain hares. A gillie I met in Central Scotland was anxious to preserve his relatively small population of hares because they were a source of food for the local eagles. The big birds might hammer the grouse stock!

The number of red grouse in the west has declined, especially since the 1920s. Over-grazing by deer and sheep has stripped moorland of its former generous coverlet of heather, a plant vital to the welfare of grouse. In some areas, a dark-green sitka spruce blanket has spread over moors where once the lively crowing of cock grouse enlivened the dawn.

Grouse have not been popular on deer forests. If you suddenly disturb a bird, it seems to explode from the heather and departs noisily. Such an alert and noisy bird gave warning to the deer, so grouse were not specially preserved, being preyed on by foxes and eagles. Many a fox cub, born in the Highlands, has used the wing or leg of a grouse as a plaything.

Years ago, the start of Highland grouse-shooting was indicated by the arrival of wealthy families, plus servants and mounds of possessions. The visitors came for a month or so. Their shooting lodges were mini-palaces, and battalions of Scotsmen left their native country to serve on the fine grouse moors of northern England. One of them gave me my first lessons in watching grouse.

A good moor produces a considerable surplus of birds, quite enough to provide a good season's sport without risk to the basic breeding stock. With the arrival of autumn, a cock bird is in good form and voice. It has fed on a variety of moorland fruits; the heather and coarse grasses are seeding. A grouse can face the coming of winter with a strong plumage and feathered legs – avian spats!

Unlike the willow grouse, of which the red is a local variant, this bird of the moors does not assume white feathers for the winter. The elevations it prefers are not high enough for this to be a necessary camouflage against glistening snowfields.

I knew a Highland poacher who went to the moors in November to call cock grouse; he lured them to within easy reach of his gun. That man would be on the moor by dawn. As the sky greyed with the coming of a new day, he listened to the crowing of a cock bird, marked its position, and – with the aid of the stem of a tobacco pipe – imitated the mewing of the hen grouse. The cock bird came over to investigate!

Grouse reared in captivity – no easy task – seem to lose their wild spirit. A gamekeeper had the misfortune to tread on a grouse nest, killing the sitting bird and several of her new-hatched chicks. The remaining chicks he slipped down his shirt, where they would be warm, and he took them home, introducing them to quarters in a large pen. That man had the wit to put in the pen some squares of heather-covered peat brought down from the moors.

The precocious chicks throve. When I saw them they were full-grown. A cock bird advanced on me with a powerful crowing and aggressive gesture. I was glad that wire netting lay between us. It was an amusing encounter, for the cock grouse yelled *go back, go back* and so did I. The bird was too close for good photography!

The experiment of hand-rearing grouse was successful only in the sense that some grouse were reared. Gone was the wild nature of the birds. They hung about the gamekeeper's house like chickens. One even perched on a window ledge. When the shooting party arrived, the keeper kept the reared grouse in an outbuilding. He had the feeling that if they had free range one would perch on the barrel of a gun!

The crowing of the cock grouse is being heard less and less on the wild moor of Rannoch. The black grouse, its larger cousin, has also declined numerically in the west. A few blackcock were present where Rannoch Moor gave way to the drier woodlands and moorland around Loch Rannoch. One day, towards the middle of May, I was motoring across the moor in declining light when I saw six blackcock, in pairs, displaying – half a dozen paces from the road!

Red grouse sort out their territorial problems in autumn. By spring – when there are further displays – the cocks are spread across the moor, entrenched in their own tracts of ground, the edges of which they seem to know to within a foot or two. Blackcock, on the other hand, assemble at a given point in spring, and their display ground is called the *lek*. Here they prance and show off their fine feathers; here they assume threat postures and sometimes fight. Each cock knows its place at the *lek*, and the behaviour is stylized; this is no rabble. Birds in the dominant positions on the ground fare best when, in due course, the coy matrons appear looking for a mate.

The glossy blue-black bodies of displaying blackcock show up against the coarse ground. When the lyre-shaped tail is raised in display, the white feathers of the under-covert form a large rosette. Feathers are puffed out, wings trail, wattles flare. Meanwhile, the birds coo and hiss as they further express the fervour of the season.

Watching birds from close quarters – a feat that is made possible when a hide is erected at the edge of the *lek* – is one of Britain's most interesting wildlife spectacles. I am impressed by the precision with which the birds occupy places on the *lek*. One bird I watched moved forward and halted abruptly, as though its legs were tied by cord to an invisible stake.

A friend who ran out a length of cable, to which a microphone was attached, hoped to record the blackcock talk. He concealed his microphone in a tuft of rushes. The birds arrived, but he noticed with dismay that the nearest pairs were nowhere near the microphone. One bird obliged him; breaking away from its partner, it advanced towards another pair and stood in the grey light and displayed. The bird called powerfully for some twenty minutes. The microphone was no more than a foot from its beak!

We found this lekking ground in autumn. Visiting blackgame country in late October, we located a number of moulted feathers. The tract of land was seen to differ slightly from that round about. At well-populated *leks* in spring, the ground vegetation is trodden down so much it resembles coconut matting.

In 1968, an American ecologist working for a period with the Nature Conservancy's grouse and moorland ecology unit fitted some blackcock with small radio transmitters. He wanted to study the birds' movements. Incidentally, this special type of transmitter weighed three-quarters of an ounce. An early discovery was that on Deeside, where the experiment was conducted, blackcock were found roosting on the ground. Tree roosting had been suspected.

I flushed some blackcock while walking along a track to the north of the Black Wood of Rannoch. When they had departed, I looked towards the wood and thought of a third species of grouse: the capercaillie. A Black Wood is black in the sense that it is composed mainly of Scots pine.

A caper in late summer and autumn can gorge itself on fruits and seeds or visit any convenient stubbles. In winter, this big bird is almost wholly dependent on pine shoots, giving rise to an idea that its flesh has a resinous tang. I am not able to confirm or deny this. No one has offered me a capercaillie sandwich! A sixteenth-century writer described the taste as "gentle".

I have already mentioned that the caper's name has been interpreted as 'the horse of the wood'. It is an inelegant way of describing a bird which is not beautiful in the accepted sense but can impress you by his size and character. A well-grown cock weighs around 12 pounds, A beard is one of the improbable features associated with this Goliath of the Scottish pinewoods for which I had looked unsuccessfully when walking near Loch Awe.

The Black Wood of Rannoch is a prime haunt of capercaillie. Gavin Johnstone and Fred Zwickel assessed the local population in 1967 as one bird per 13–16 acres. I strode through the wood in the late afternoon, enjoying that sort of peace I associate with a tour of a large cathedral. Trees rose on either side of the path for 40 or 50 feet. The finest trees are about 80 feet high, as straight as ships' masts.

The quietness enabled me to locate a cock capercaillie at the moment it burst noisily from a tree and moved off at a high speed, its neck extended. Strong wingbeats propelled it to an acceptable pace, and then it shut off the power for a while, as the red grouse had done on the open moor. The big bird glided, swerving this way and that to avoid tree trunks. I have known startled capercaillie to ignore lesser growth; they simply barged through it!

In the mating season, the cock caper greets a new day with a bizarre song. A ticking sound (somewhat like the sound of a horse's hooves, I suppose) leads to a curious miscellany of calls and culminates in a pop such as you hear when a cork is removed from a champagne bottle!

The hen bird is smaller, less prominent, with a reddish patch to her breast. When on the nest, she squats without a blink or tremble, relying on total immobility to avoid detection. Once when I found a sitting hen in a pinewood, I tested the bird's reputation as a close-sitter by advancing to a given point, some four yards away. I had decided that if the bird flew off, I would briefly examine the nest. If she remained, I would immediately walk away.

She remained! The image in my telephoto lens grew larger and larger. At four yards I saw my reflection in the bird's lustrous eyes. I wished her well – and walked away.

A hen bird turned on me when I picked up one of a brood of lusty young capers that were crossing a forest road. I associate aggression with the cock bird, a few of which can be nasty towards human visitors. The bird raises the large feathers of its tail until they are like a fan, against which the bright wattles on the head show up vividly; and then it advances. I would advise anyone who sees a bird displaying thus to turn and run!

Hen capercaillie are the first to prospect new country; they are seen about two years before the cock birds appear and may, indeed, have mated with the local blackcock. Hybrids are not uncommon.

As I left the Black Wood when it was almost dark, I stopped the car as a capercaillie crossed the road. The bird moved with a regal disdain for the vehicle.

17

Highland Reds

A few thousand years ago – merely a wink in the story of the land – the ancestors of our red deer re-established themselves in the Highlands. They arrived in the wake of retreating ice, moving into a landscape that bore the fresh wounds of glaciation.

Deer that spread slowly northwards as conditions moderated and the land began to heal itself, were larger, fuller in the frame, than the type of red deer we see living on the poor treeless hills of today. Generations of deer, untroubled by man, could then summer on the grassy hilltops and descend in rigorous weather to open woodland.

Megaceros, or the Irish elk, a deer that was mightier than the red, throve on the grassy plains of inter-glacial periods. A full-grown stag stood at over six feet. Its head was decked by palmated antlers weighing up to 19 pounds. This great beast may have shuffled from the Highland scene before the first men appeared. As Peter Delap has written, "it priced itself out of the evolutionary rat-race".

Long-term climatic rhythms caused dramatically visible marks on the landscape. The Highlands had been smothered by snow and ice.

In warmer conditions, the ice melted and tundra appeared. Trees spread into the wilderness with a surprising speed, and eventually birch and pine were present on higher ground, with hardwoods developing in the glens. Peat, forming in cold and soggy conditions, overwhelmed and buried many an ancient upland forest.

The red deer regulated their lives according to the season, the weather – and the wolf, a principal predator. The evening air shivered as wolf packs re-formed for hunting, which they undertook by scent and not by sight. A wolf might not succeed in outpacing a red deer in its prime, but it could – and did – cull the very young, the infirm and the old.

No creature troubled the wolf until man arrived, first as small parties of hunters and fisherman, then as families who settled and began the forest clearance. The wolf threatened a farmer's domesticated animals and so the wolf must go. It was flushed from woodland cover by men who took the dramatic course of burning down the trees. Early in the eighteenth century, a few demoralized wolves remained. Their social system had collapsed. The Scottish wolf became extinct about 1743.

A stalker named Macqueen, whose home was by the Findhorn, is credited with slaying the last Caledonian Wolf, and he described the incident thus: "As I came through the slochk by east the hill there, I foregathered wi' the beast. My long dog there turned him. I buckled wi' him, and dirkit him, and syne whuttled his craig, and brought his countenance for fear he should come alive again, for they are precarious creatures . . ."

The memory of wolves remains in folk tales that have been passed on for many generations. The European mind was conditioned to fear the wolf, and this fear was taken to the New World by early European settlers. The wolf had for so long been adversary of the Highland red deer, it is possible that they retained impressions of the creature long after the wolf departed.

The red deer haunted the dreams of early man. Each deer slain represented a few hundred pounds of fresh lean meat, which was a welcome addition to the winter diet. As the forests declined for a variety of reasons, and as many a hill became bare, the deer population was reduced. By adapting themselves to changing circumstances, the deer themselves had become smaller than their ancestors. A bare, acid hill with hardly any shelter against the weather is unlikely to produce outstanding stock.

Was the red deer ever, exclusively, a woodlander? Peter Delap has written: "Had the red deer been true forest dwellers they could never have survived upon the treeless wastes of the far north. The more one studies their habits and social relationships, the more obvious it becomes that the red deer, able to exploit any available habitat, is a tree-line, marginal species and not a woodlander as commonly categorised."

The hunting of deer by people who craved for fresh protein
– a craving we who are overfed today cannot truly understand
– developed in time into deer drives, or *tainchels*, organized by
the chiefs to replenish the larder and maybe at the same time
impress an important visitor.

A chief sent the lustiest of his people across the hills to flush
the deer, which then were directed into an area that favoured
the hunter. A bloodbath ensued. Some exaggerated accounts
were given of the number of deer slain. The places where deer
were regularly driven are indicated on the map by the element
elrig in a place-name.

The imaginative Celtic folk who arrived from the west
imbued the landscape and its deer with intense feeling. Consider this poetic expression of tenderness towards the native
land:

> I see the ridge of hinds, the steep of the sloping glen,
> The wood of cuckoos at its foot,
> The blue height of a thousand pines.

Celtic folk may have brought with them the large, shaggy
hound used for deer-hunting. It was a large but lithesome
animal, standing about 28 inches at the shoulder, clad in a wiry
grey coat. A hound named Bran belonged to the mighty Fingal.

The Gael put into rhyme an exaggerated idea about
mammalian ages, and – of course – he included the red deer:

> Thrice the age of a dog, the age of a horse;
> Thrice the age of a horse, the age of a man;
> Thrice the age of a man, the age of a stag;
> Thrice the age of a stag, the age of an eagle;
> Thrice the age of an eagle, the age of an oak tree.

So stern is life on the open hill that a red stag is a veteran at
fifteen; and many deer live to nowhere near that age. The
process of degradation of the hill by forest clearance is difficult
to reverse; changes come to the upland soils through leaching.
They become increasingly acid. The terrain of red deer was
both bleak and poor in keep.

Came the sheep – thousands of sheep, spreading out across

the glens and up the hills as Highland lairds leased the land to flockmasters from the Borders. The teeth of many sheep mowed the landscape so finely that natural regeneration of woodland was difficult; the sheep also benefited from the rich sward on soil that had formed for centuries under forest conditions. The richness could not last, and sheep walks began to deteriorate. With a diminished revenue from sheep, the Highland laird wondered where his next source of income would be. At about this time, the stalking of deer was becoming a popular sport.

Lord Dulverton has related that before stalking was really popular, the guardian to Lord Lovat advised his charge not to so far derogate from his position as to think of going into the forest to shoot deer for himself, a practice that was neither dignified nor customary in a gentleman.

It was an attitude that changed. References to stalking deer began to appear in the eighteenth century, but not until the nineteenth century did the fashion have the financial support of a host of wealthy men in a position to rent a forest for sport. Two influential people at the time were Scrope, who wrote about days spent deer-stalking, and Queen Victoria (not forgetting Albert) who established a Highland home at Balmoral.

Scrope's book (to which further reference will be made) is a lively account of a more precise form of sport than the deer-drive. He wrote engagingly of high hills, wild deer and the new folk-hero, the stalker, who "should be able to run in a stooping position, at a greyhound pace, with his back parallel to the ground and his face within an inch of it, for miles altogether".

Victoria's prose and sketches indicated her love for Highland sport, especially when dear Albert was involved. She wrote in 1852: "Albert had already killed the stag; and in the road he lay . . . the beauty we had admired yesterday evening. He was a magnificent animal, and I sat down and scratched a little sketch of him . . . What a delightful day!" Some cosy little customs developed. When a stag was shot in Ballochbuie, Victoria noted: "I was supposed to have 'a lucky foot', of which the Highlanders think a geat deal."

The sport of deer-stalking was for the select few: those with plenty of money. The rich were not then beset by heavy taxation. With the coming of autumn, many of them happily left London, or country estates in the south, or northern industrial towns, for the days of fresh air and healthy exercise in the Highlands. The Industrial Revolution had created a new class of wealthy men; having built up fortunes, they were anxious to spend in a way that would impress their friends and associates.

The increasing popularity of deer-stalking was also stimulated by the improved designs of guns. When the crackle of gunfire was not being heard in the deer forests, a great hush descended on the hills. A hill without sheep is a quiet place, and sheep had been driven away from the best areas.

In 1833, Charles St John contributed a book to the sporting literature of the Highlands. He mentioned his pursuit of the "Muckle Hart of Benmore", a task spread over six days. This hunter was tough; at night, when there was no handy shelter he and his companions wrapped their plaids around them, "and slept pretty comfortably".

The Highlands were again prosperous. Roads and bridges were made to link up roads with the lodges built at remote glenheads. Many of the lodges were palatial – a blend of English, French, even German styles. A surprisingly large number looked like Balmoral! All this work created jobs for Highland men. Many a wife or daughter had seasonal work in 'the big hoose'.

Shooting tenants arrived with their large families, small armies of servants and gargantuan luggage. They installed themselves in rooms with panelled walls, fireplaces adorned with painted tiles, and substantial furniture. They lived here under beady eyes, set in stuffed deer heads. They found novelty in sitting on seats fashioned entirely from deer antlers.

The rich visitor awoke, washed and dressed, had his breakfast, then strode out into the crisp mountain air to see the glory of the Highlands in autumn, to hear the babble of many burns, the burr of voices as stalker addressed gillie, and gillie had a word or two with the humble pony boy.

At home, the visiting tycoon was accustomed to issuing orders that were instantly obeyed. Now he meekly allowed himself to be taken to the heights and coaxed over peat slabs, between rocks and along dark and sloppy gutters by the local men. He shot his stag, then returned to the lodge, his face glowing from the effects of unaccustomed fresh air, his muscles stiff from unaccustomed exercise. He would bathe, change into evening dress and saunter into the hall for 'wee drams' and talk. The exploits of the day were related – and adorned a little by imaginative presentation.

Aristocrat, city banker, mill-owner shared a common experience and could not return home fast enough to tell their friends about it.

To the Victorian sportsman, the 'head' was the main topic of sporting conversation. He was obsessed with the size, weight and proliferation of 'points' on a deer's antlers. Trophy-hunting was the thing. The best stags were shot. To secure a good stock, the Highland reds were cossetted as never before, and given nourishing rations to augment the coarse hill fare in winter. They were crossed with English park stags, German stags, even the wapiti, the red deer's cousin from North America.

When the visitors had returned to their homes down south, the long-suffering stalkers were left to deal with culling the hinds. If there were too many hinds, the finest stags in the forest were incapable of covering them all. Consequently, a poorer class of stag had his way.

No one worried about the effect that this sporting gluttony was having on the Highland ecology. At that time, only a few people were aware of the delicate interplay of natural forces that leads to a healthy landscape. Stocking rates of deer became ridiculously high. Nutrients were leached from bare hillsides by heavy rain and incessant grazing by deer. Moorland was fired to destroy the rank old heather and to encourage the growth of a fresh 'bite' for grouse, sheep and deer. And so the hills remained devoid of trees, except where odd specimens managed to develop between rocks or on cliffs that were inaccessible to stock.

The first economic setback for the Highlands came during the 1914-18 war, when many deer forests were unlet, and deer were shot for food. At a time of food scarcity, sheep and cattle returned to many hills. The pattern repeated itself in the 1939-45 war.

By this time, a new force was influencing the Highland landscape. So savage was the assault on Britain's woodlands and forests for timber needed for the war effort, that after the First World War the Forestry Commission was established, charged with replenishing our reserves.

Many glens were flooded by the hydro-electricity authority. So the red deer came up against fences that prevented access to the new plantations, and descending the hill in grim weather, they found that many of the lowland flats, where grazing had been good, were now covered with water.

The Highland red deer survives and in quite large numbers. The population of red deer in Scotland is estimated to be 180,000, most of the animals being found in the Highland zone. The Scottish deer forest remains as a special type of sporting landscape. Sportsmen from the continent rejoice in what to them are novel conditions – open hill, abundant deer. Most of the Highland venison is consigned to Germany.

Highland estates are suffering – as we all suffer – from the effects of inflation and high taxation. The number of workers has been greatly reduced. The number of stalkers has declined, which is a pity, for in the stalker's mind reposes all the know-how of a locality – its geography, traditions, natural history, even folklore.

The stalker has enhanced the Highland life for 150 years. He has been – at most times – a solitary figure on the landscape. Many a stalker has lived alone, miles from the nearest habitation, for a man who could persuade a woman to share his life back o' beyond was doubly blessed.

As for the deer, their high country is no longer peaceful. Hill-walkers by the hundred disturb them at their daytime lies. I suppose they have become accustomed to the whine of jet aircraft.

The red deer have their place, wrote Lord Dulverton in the *Journal* of the British Deer Society. "Over large tracts of barren mountain it is an important place because the deer are better than any other livestock at utilising the mountain herbage and environment, and can convert very poor stuff, including the lichens and sour bog grasses, into high protein food for humans."

A few thousand years ago – merely a wink in the story of the land – the ancestors of our red deer re-established themselves in the Highlands after the turbulence of the last Ice Age. Some scientists believe we are, even now, in an inter-glacial period. If the ice sheets spread again, man and deer will be forced to move southwards. It is almost certain that the deer will return before man to the northern hills . . . .

18

Scrope's Way

May I reintroduce William Scrope, Victorian deer-stalker? I renewed my acquaintance with him one evening while browsing through my host's collection of Scottish books. Here was *Days of Deer-Stalking,* published in 1845. I read the work at a single sitting that extended into the wee small hours. When it was done, my eyes prickled with fatigue but my mind retained a galaxy of impressions of life in the Highlands.

A Sassenach, William Scrope spent ten happy, healthful years in the Forest of Atholl. In his day, the red stag was regarded as so much protein on the hoof. The sight of it activated a man's gastric juices rather than his sporting instincts. The Earl of Malmesbury wrote in his *Memoirs* in 1833: "This was the first year that the Highlands became the rage and that deer forests were made and rented, but for prices not exceeding £300 a year." In 1834, according to Anderson's *Guide to Scotland,* "It has now become a common practice for Highland proprietors to let the right of shooting over their ground. Moors may be had at all prices from £50 to £500 for the season, with accommodation varying according to circumstances."

The real development of deer-stalking was greatly influenced by Scrope's book; he was the prophet of a new sporting age – and like all good prophets he cried out in the wilderness! He described day-long tramps with rifle, shot, powder-flask, whisky, pony and "high-couraged dogs of various breeds". The idea of stalking was to outwit the deer, specific deer, and glory in the achievement.

He took his stag nomenclature from that being used by a Devonshire hunt. He experimented with the breeding of dogs, crossing a greyhound with a foxhound to get both speed and 'nose'.

To many of the dour Scotsmen he met, Scrope must have

appeared wildly eccentric. The English visitor was seen in many unusual forms. Scrope told of two or three visiting sportsmen who "discharged their rifles at the gillies' bonnets, at a distance of a hundred paces, the gillies wisely pulling them off and planting them in the heather . . . . ".

The new techniques were explained in the context of lively accounts of outings in and around Glen Tilt. Learning by the Scrope method was pleasurable. Every page was spiced with humour, and prose raced along. He set down as much as was known about the biologs of the red deer, and he exposed – always with quiet courtesy – some of the fallacies. He introduced the reader to the (comparatively few) deer forests, gave historical notes on early field sports, Highland legends, superstitions, traditions, folklore, poachers and free-booters.

The stalker did not go out because he was hungry; nevertheless, Scrope exulted when there was well-cooked venison for dinner. We are told that "almost every part of the deer is excellent for the table: the liver, the heart, the tripe, the feet, and the white puddings, should not be neglected". Scrope sent a haunch of venison to his friend, Sir Walter Scott, who replied:

> Thanks, dear Sir, for your venison, for finer or fatter
> Never roam'd in a forest, or smoked in a platter.

Scrope was quick-witted and observant. After breakfast he said to a companion: "I see by the course of the clouds which I have been watching from my bed that the wind is in the right airt, and as the weather is warm the deer will be far out on the tops of the hills."

He observed what modern students of red deer call the animal's 'plastic quality' – an ability speedily to adjust its size to local conditions, so that the beast on the poorest Scottish hills may be only half the weight of a pampered stag in a South Country deer park. "Such stags as have, for the most part, abandoned the Scotch mountains, and pastured in the large woods in the low country, have been found considerably to exceed the hill stags in size and condition," he wrote.

He remarked that deer with few points to their antlers were sometimes larger and fatter than those with many branches, and

Wet evening at Rannoch Station. The railway line had to be 'floated' on the moorland bogs.

Snow-dusted bens loom beyond a lochan at the edge of Rannoch Moor.

Scots pines. The species formed an important part of the old Caledonian Forest.

Above: A park red stag roaring. The hill stag of the Highlands may only be half the weight, and have a far less imposing head, than such a beast as this.

Below: Sparring between red stags in a deer park. The clatter of antlers as they are locked together is a feature of the Highland autumn.

Above right: A red stag and his harem at the time of the rut.

Below right: Nose in the air, a red stag offers a threat display to a rival at the time of the rut.

Sir Walter Scott at Loch Katrine. The author is commemorated by the name of this fine pleasure craft.

Highland cattle and a deer pony below Ben More in Glen Dochart.

A dead tree on Rannoch Moor.

"if the impression of a deer's foot measures full two inches at the heel, he is warrantable; if three inches, and the hoofs mark deeply in the ground, allowing for its nature, he is a large heavy old deer".

Stags carry their horns "just as long as the hind carries her fawn, which is eight months . . . Hinds that have calves have no fat whatever upon them, and are fit only for soup, or perhaps for stewing".

Scrope, ever-sensitive to atmosphere, became almost delirious in the autumn when the deer were demonstrative. At the time of the rut,

> the harts swell in their necks, have a ruff of long wiry hair about them, and are drawn up in their bodies like greyhounds. They now roll restlessly in the peat pools till they become almost black with mire, and feed chiefly on a light-coloured moss that grows on the round tops of the hills, so that they do not differ so entirely from the reindeer in their food as some naturalists have imagined.

In autumn, the harts "are heard roaring all over the forest, and are engaged in savage conflicts with each other, which sometimes terminate fatally". Sporting artists like Edwin Landseer conditioned the general public to the idea that red stags spend most of their time fighting each other, whereas a threat gesture by one stag to a challenger is frequently enough of a deterrent. Or the stag runs towards a hesitant challenger with loud bleating. Landseer provided a frontispiece and vignette for Scrope's book. Lithographs in the volume were from drawings by Charles Landseer.

We must now revise some of Scrope's ideas, but generally his views are more credible than many that were expressed in his day. And he did not blindly accept all that was told to him. A popular story of the time concerned the Earl of Atholl who, when host to Queen Mary, sent out some 2,000 Highlanders to gather the deer, a task over which they spent weeks, and eventually 2,000 red deer were slain "beside roes, does, and other game". Scrope was rightly sceptical.

Stalking the red deer was made possible by improvements in the manufacture of firearms. Scrope tells us that firearms were unknown in Sutherland until about the latter part of the six-

teenth century, when a large and awkward type of blunderbuss
was obtained by Angus Baillie of Uppat. It was believed that
the gun came from the wreck of a Spanish galleon in 1584.
Guns used in the far north were still very crude during the
early part of the seventeenth century, a barrel being attached to
the stock by iron hoops. Deer were being regularly slain by
bow and arrow. Earlier, a wounded deer was despatched by a
thrust from a spear.

Wild as a Highland deer forest might look, the features were
known in considerable detail. Every rock, corrie, cairn and
mountain had a distinctive name, and there were many sub-
divisions so that a precise spot could be indicated by name.
"The men appointed to bring home the dead deer, being told
where they lay, never failed to find them."

The intending stalker was urged to wear durable clothes, for
the weather was subject to sudden variations and could be
uncomfortable. Of Scotch mist, he wrote: "These clouds of mist
are sure to last some hours, or may continue the whole
morning, and finally terminate in a deluge of everlasting rain."

Footwear should be either thick shoes with nails or Scottish
brogues. Sportsmen were advised to "take care that the ramrod
to your rifles be large and strong; it will otherwise be broken in
the hurry of loading".

Scrope's narratives contain quotations in which local men are
made to speak in a vaguely Scottish way – vaguely because the
author used a number of Perthshire words that were neither
strictly of the Highlands nor had a Lowland character. The
expressions used do include a picturesque reference to dawn as
"the skreek o' day".

Every man knew his social position. Peter Fraser frequently
touched his cap. But nobles and kerns mixed fairly freely on the
hill because they had common interests. Inevitably, the Scot of
the Highland estate was portrayed in a slightly comic vein. We
are given a picture of men soiled and heated with toil, wearing
blue bonnets and plaided kilts. One of them, told not to forget
the whisky, replies in droll fashion: "Na, na, I aye tak tent o'
that. Did ye ever knaw me lave it ahint?" When a good stag
is seen, the native observes – quietly, of course – "Ou, what
a bowkit beast!"

Scrope's originality of expression is evidenced in his des-
cription of a place as "about eight reputed miles north of Blair
Atholl, which distance would be numbered ten in a country of
milestones". At other times he tends to 'go on a bit', as for
example:

> Perhaps it is impolitic to raise your expectations as to the chase;
> and, indeed, it is impossible for me to describe the enthusiasm I felt
> when I first began my career. In the pursuit, the stag's motions are
> so noble, and his reasoning so acute, that, believe me, I had rather
> follow one hart from morning till night with the expectation of
> getting a shot (in which I might be properly defeated) than have
> the best day's sport with moor fowl that the hills could afford me.
> All your powers of body and mind are called into action, and if
> they are not properly exercised, the clever creature will inevitably
> defeat you: it is quite an affair of generalship . . .

We go with him to the hills. The ground is scanned through
a telescope. In view are a few hinds, but no hart. Then a stalker
"has a blink of a hart lying in the bog by the burn". They close
on the stag, following an unpleasant and difficult route. A shot
is fired, and crack goes the ball right against the animal's ribs as
he is making his rush. Two dogs are released to prevent the
stag from going to the hill, but he goes over a ridge out of sight,
and after it the hounds.

The hunters find the stag standing on a ledge of rock within
a cleft; the rock is in the mid course of a burn. The dogs bay
furiously. It is time to shoot again, to despatch the wounded
beast. The stag is bled, opened, gralloched. The men turn the
stag's head back on his shoulder, cover the deer with peats,
shake over him a little gunpowder, and tie a black flag to his
horns. The idea is to scare away the scavenger ravens. A few
peats are heaped up in a conspicuous place, a little way from the
stag's body, to mark the spot where he lies.

Stalking became ritualized. So did the ancient Scottish art of
poaching. Two methods used by poachers were described. A
solitary man would hang about watching the keepers; he moved
in for a kill when an opportunity came. In the other method,
gangs of marauders went from forest to forest; they bedded
down in a bothy or even in an unoccupied shooting lodge.

Because these men operated at the end of the usual stalking season, the harts were entirely rank and useless, but the yeld [barren] hinds came in at that period, "and are very fine venison; and all the other hinds make the best possible soup, and are very good hill-man's eating, though they are totally devoid of fat".

A poaching gang lived on the venison they could not sell. The men drank vast quantities of whisky and were fond of tobacco. "They must pass a very pleasant wandering life". mused Scrope. A gang was discouraged if attacked in the bothy at night. Scrope tells us that Chisholm's Cave "in the Ben Kilbreck forest, in Sutherland", derives its name from that of a freebooter who passed his life in caverns, "poaching and living on pillage".

We are given details of the old Scottish greyhound, a type still owned by Scottish gentlemen and chiefs. The best sort of dog for chasing the deer was the original Scotch or Irish greyhound, but this breed was now scarce. Scrope was informed that in Sutherland the last of the race in that particular district was a powerful animal belonging to the late Mr Gordon of Achness. The hound had been killed by a stag about forty years before. The deer 'transfixed him with his antlers against a rock, leaving three deadly wounds on his body".

Ponies are introduced to the reader. The hardy Highland garron was "redundant in mane and tail, and contemner of the bridle". The eagle was considered by Scrope to be a villain, a murderer. A small herd boy, he reported with glee, was seen staggering along near Abergeldie with two eagles, "which he held by the necks", over his shoulders.

Scrope's lyricism would send a shiver of pleasure down the spines of his readers. As, for example:

The deer were now urged on in beautiful style from the Beg of Cairn Bairg. It was like the passage of a little army as their files drew on; were lost in the hollows, re-appearing and again sinking out of sight amidst the mazes of the moor. Nothing could be more picturesque than their undulating course – nothing more gratifying than to reckon the horns marked firmly on the skyline as they passed over the summits.

Such pictures were in the forefront of my mind when, having finished the old book in a quiet lounge, I went off to bed for what turned out to be an uneasy sleep.

19

A Time for Roaring

An October evening, somewhere in Argyll. Darkness comes
early, and the temperature plummets. There is no wind to sear
any exposed flesh, but the frosty air brings a tingling sensation
to my ears, and a purple cast to my hands, as I walk back across
the hill. My legs feel so stiff that I fancy my knee joints are
creaking.

I had gone to the hill to sample the last hour of daylight. A
hen harrier appeared, patrolling the hill edge for food. An
unseen hooded crow – I presumed it was a 'whoodie' – honked
like an old-fashioned motor horn. From a farm came the urgent
yapping of a dog.

Then the busy world was hushed. It was that kind of silence
that falls over a theatre audience as the orchestral conductor
holds up his baton. The silence of expectancy.

I heard a throaty roar – deep, resonant, not especially loud
but with great carrying power. A stranger might have imagined
that a cow was bawling for a lost calf, but the sound emanated
from the throat box of a Highland red stag, monarch of hill and
glen. I saw the big shaggy beast and noticed that near it was a
group of hinds and calves.

The season of roaring begins traditionally on 26 September.
The lusty call of a stag is a warning to other stags: keep away!
Hearing it on the hill in Argyll I thought of other occasions on
which I heard a stag give voice – on the wastes of Mar in upper
Deeside and in the echo chamber of upper Glen Feshie; across
the rock wastes of Torridon and from a hillside above Kinloch
on the isle of Rhum.

A friend with a job in the Highlands left his lodgings one
evening to visit a phone box and chat with an acquaintance in
Fort William. It was the time of roaring. Several stags were
clearly visible to him as he stood in the phone box. One stag

was so loudly vocal that the man could scarcely hear what his friend was saying. So he excused himself, left the box, picked up a tussock of grass and earth, and hurled it at the stag!

The red stag, like the fox, finds its voice at mating time. The rut is the heady climax of a year spent mainly in feeding and resting. A red deer's year is eventful . . .

A hind carries her calf through a gestation period of eight months; this includes the bitter winter. In many years, early spring is even more bitter and she moves through a landscape crusted with snow and ice. In the absence of tree cover, she drops the calf on a peat hag or among tussocks of heather. Weakly calves die; so do a number of unlucky infants taken by fox or eagle when the hind is absent. But sufficient calves are reared to do more than maintain the deer population. A calf is soon following the hind across the lush summer pastures. It is then that the adult red deer is truly red.

The sexes stay apart, with their own routine of grazing and lying up to rest. By July, the stags have grown fresh antlers to replace those cast in spring. The deer calf becomes plain of appearance as the white-dappled coat becomes darker. The dappling had helped to break up the outline of the calf's chunky form in infancy.

In summer, deer tend to stay high up the hill, to be spared the torment of insect pests. The calf is in its first winter coat in September, which is the time when the stags begin to roar. Then, for a month, the stags join the females, each claiming as many as he can.

A rutting stag can look fearsome, for his antlers may be adorned with sods and strands of hill grass picked up as he threshes the ground vegetation. His neck is covered by a shaggy mane. He may have recently rolled in a porridge-like mixture of peaty mud; if so, his legs and the lower part of his body will be crusted with dark earth that glistens in daylight.

The beast that roared for me was a true hill type, fairly small of stature, weighing perhaps 15 stone. From the moment of his birth to adulthood he had known only the rigours of life on the open hill – the short rations of spring, the dust and flies of summer drought and the soggy cheerlessness of summer spate; the mists and frosty nip of autumn and the snows of winter.

By now, his powerful roaring reverberated through the district. He stopped to rub himself against a boulder. An amusing story is told of a Duke of Argyll who, realizing that his hill deer had no trees against which they might rub or clean their horns, asked his workforce to erect poles. Later, a tramp was seen rubbing his back ecstatically against a roadside post, remarking: "God bless the Duke of Argyll."

A well-run stag develops a 'nipped in' appearance; he maintains such a level of excitement he cannot settle down to feed and eventually his stomach contains a small quantity of dark liquid. The nervous energy expended contributes to his sad plight. He is constantly on patrol, herding the hinds, driving off rivals. If a competitor appears, he roars lustily or, at close range, makes a sudden dash towards the intruder; with head up, he utters an urgent bleating.

He also smells strongly! We know scarcely anything about the fine odours from deer glands which must play an important role in their communal life, though during the deer rut there is an easily detectable heavy smell of stag at the wallows.

The animal I had under scrutiny would not keep his hinds much longer. He may have started the rut as a 15-stone stag, his body well nourished by the rich summer grazing. He would end it as lean as a whippet! I watched him pursue a hind, his tongue lolling from his mouth. The hind was not in season, and she evaded him with ease and the use of a graceful skipping action.

The small group of deer wandered to a stand of pine trees. Here the stag lowered his head to rub his antlers vigorously against a trunk. When he had moved away, one hind approached with considerable excitement, standing a little way off, but stretching out her neck to sniff the wood. Then she advanced on the tree and rubbed against it for a minute or so, working slowly, ecstatically.

Mercifully for me, the midge season was over. Any late midges would be frost-bitten! Hill deer face all manner of insect pests – ticks, keds, warbles. The latter infect them in summer so that when a stalker skins a culled hind in winter he may find that the skin has many holes – the exits by which the warbles left the body.

I sat among rushes, viewing a basin between hills, noticing that near the centre of the basin was a tree-covered knoll. I had earlier established that a big wallow lay beyond.

The hinds and proprietorial stag were in the open again. A young hind is not sexually attractive until she is two years old and – coming into season – is receptive for a short time. If she is not covered then, she will return to mating condition a few weeks later.

Generally speaking, the red deer rut is short and intense. It is virtually over by the end of October, though the last hind may come into season in the early part of November.

Hinds arrive on the rutting grounds a week or so before the stags. The ground I was surveying had heard its first stag roar about 19 September, said a local stalker, who quietly joined me. The stalker reached for his telescope and located three young stags grazing high on the hill. One stag was dark and wet. He had been wallowing.

The stalker turned towards the master stag, cupped his hands over his mouth and called: "Uh, uh, eerh!"

Every deer raised its head.

"That should get the old stag started," said the stalker. "The ruse works best if you call into a newspaper that's been rolled up like a trumpet."

The big stag roared back and began to gather up the hinds. He was a ten-point stag, with wide head and double brow tines.

The stalker called again. A low sound, it wavered a little. The big stag responded with a single, short call. It sounded deep, dry.

"Uh, uh, eerr," called the stalker, and the stag responded, looking directly at us over a considerable area of hill. Then the stag began to move towards us. Or so we thought.

"He's not a terribly big stag, though he's a nice body," said the stalker, adding – for the stag's benefit – "uuuuurgh!"

The stag's next call was at a low pitch. He began to lope towards us, The stag roared; his head went up and the mouth opened until it looked like a dark 'O'. The afterglow of the sun burnished the stag's glossy flanks. Coming closer, he increased his speed, virtually walking over a wire fence.

A roar was uttered from much closer range – a matter of 200

yards. Here, and so far undetected by us, stood a stag with six points to his antlers. He was youngish, but managed to produce a succession of deep bellows. His voice must have broken early.

All went quiet. The challenge to the master was not maintained.

A stag might claim a large group of hinds at the start of the rut; the number tends to decline as more stags arrive and manage to herd off some of the females. The first master has to abdicate, which may be done voluntarily when a stag, exhausted by a gruelling wardenship, withdraws from the battlefield, or when he is beaten in conflict.

Victorian artists loved to portray fighting stags. This method of resolving a difference is a last resort. But, as I have indicated, a rival is usually demoralized when the master uses threat gestures. Highland stags can undoubtedly injure themselves when fighting, and I have seen more than one that was blinded in the eye when the brow point of a rival was placed unfortunately. A stag I knew blinded itself when rubbing his head against barbed wire.

Usually, a conflict between stags is little more than a pushing match. It is always dramatic, however, and a human hears a dry rattle – a sound rather like that produced when two walking sticks are clashed together – as the antlers collide.

The big stag silenced his young rival without resort to fighting. After advancing on the youngster, he looked back up the hill, where the hinds had last been. And he slowly went back to them, via the three young stags, which he banished from the area. One of them did stand its ground, but when the old chap ran towards it the other deer took to his heels.

"Uh, uh, err, ergh!" called the stalker, and the sound brought a response from the six-point stag. He looked towards us and raised his head to give voice. Then he came towards us, in stages. At 120 yards, the stalker coaxed another round of roaring from him. Concurrently, the big stag up the hill bellowed his annoyance.

The young stag moved closer to us with mounting excitement. He tossed his head. Standing broadside to us, at about sixty yards, he roared and again shook his head as though to dissipate some surplus nervous energy. The big stag roared in the distance.

When the young stag identified us as humans, he strode haughtily away. We glanced up the hill, which now was vacant. The main group of deer had moved into woodland cover.

Watching deer in woodland is more difficult than on the open hill, as you would suppose. Frequently you cannot see the deer for the trees. A friend telephoned to say that when he had been preparing for bed at about 11 p.m. the previous day, he heard a stag call from one of several big wooded crags. Opening his bedroom window, my friend listened to a sound half as old as time.

The night was calm and rather cool. He was aware only of the black mass of the hills. A big stag roared again, and the surrounding crags gave to the roar an effect such as is attained in an echo-chamber.

The rut had begun poorly, with unaccustomed hot weather to retard this peak-of-the-year performance. A month before, he observed the deer as being fit and healthy after the lush summer grazing. They were moving in quite large groups, one area holding up to twenty, mainly hinds, calves and yearlings.

I went with my friend to the wooded heights. We used a forestry road, at the side of which lay evidence of the pre-rut season: young, regenerating larch that were badly frayed. The road levelled out at over 1,200 feet. On one side the ground fell steeply away to where a burn ran white with the effects of recent rain. Beyond, the ground climbed steeply again and was fleshed with thin acid soil that supported nothing more appetizing than bracken and poor quality grasses, terminating in crags around which a raven glided and called.

On the road's other side, the air was heady with the scent of conifer resin – a tang that was all the stronger because the air was still and warm. It was also very wet!

We had seen only four deer at this stage of the excursion. A six-point stag sprinted off, stopped, and looked back at us. Three hinds were in attendance, of which one was a yearling. We relocated the stag when we were much higher than he was: we saw that his coat was still very summery, and that the reddish hue blended well with the bare earth around. The animal had chosen to stop on ground that was recently clear-felled.

We had been watching the stag for five minutes when we realized that the three hinds were in attendance. They stood, bunched, attentive, but not moving a muscle, blending with the open ground, and detectable because they had lightly toned discs on their rumps and light hair at the rims of their ears.

Five hinds used the freezing technique in moderate cover, and we almost overlooked them as we strode by. The oldest hind was wise to the ways of the world and of men. She, not he, is the leader of red deer society; it is basically matriarchal. With this hind was a slightly younger female; also two yearlings and calf.

My friend led me from the unmetalled roadway and up a bank adorned by heather and grasses. The fiery tones of autumn were upon them. Among the small conifers were dead specimens that stood cocooned in a silver fuzz, a form of lichen.

We moved forward a few yards at a time. My friend's posture stiffened. He looked fixedly ahead. Raising myself slowly above the near horizon, I looked at a bank of trees. Against them were two hinds and a calf of the year. A large stag, sporting ten points to the antlers, materialized at the edge of the plantation; it was like a transformation scene at a pantomime, for I had not seen or heard him as he emerged from cover. There was a disfigurement to the left antler; a brow tine was missing.

The hinds and youngster departed, among Norway spruce. We viewed the stag from only thirty yards, and he stared towards us. As he raised his head to taste the air, a white ring around the muzzle was clearly seen. For a moment, we thought he might advance threateningly upon us, but then he turned and departed. It was not a wild rush but a regal gait. It was as though he was informing us that he held this hill by the right of many generations. We were the intruders.

We found ourselves in an area where wallowing took place. During the rut, stags take mud baths for a variety of reasons, one of them being to cool their ardour. Also, by plastering themselves with mud, they seek to look more fearsome to their rivals. Another reason will be a desire to spread their distinctive smell around their rutting ground. There is always a strong, rank scent at a wallow in October.

The wallows were great baths, some along the course of a burn, others excavated under the canopies of conifers. All were brimful with water. It had been raining steadily since dawn! In one wallow, recently used, the water was clouded; it was now a khaki mixture, resembling wet oatmeal.

Some wallows testified by their size to a deer's enormous surfeit of energy. Younger stags, caught up in the excitement of the season, may wallow too, emulating the masters – when these were not present! Few wallows are made in summer, when overheated red deer tend to cool off by plunging into pools in the burns.

As we stared at a boggy area that was pockmarked by great wallows, we were suddenly conscious of being overlooked. Twenty yards away stood a stag; it was among the trees, its head concealed, but it must have been a big boy.

Had he heard the crackling of twigs as we moved? Did he think we were rival deer? The animal moved quietly away.

We broke out of tree cover and looked at the next range of wooded hills. They were only faintly visible in the mist and the rain. We entered a larch wood where the ground sloped steeply. Yet because the trees were set at reasonable distances from each other, we could look far.

A three-year-old stag wandered aimlessly ahead of us, as though he had turned up too early for an appointment. He was a 'switch', with unbranched antlers. Switches can be deadly, for the antler formation gives the owner a considerable advantage even over a much larger stag. These horns were long, narrow, sharp at the tip – curving rapiers.

We saw hinds moving far below. There were maybe eight animals. Some lay cud-chewing; the active ones grazed. It was a matter of urgency to locate the old hind, the most experienced and attentive; we must not come within her eager gaze.

In the end, the old hind saw me. She gave a warning call. I watched an exodus of female deer. The attendant big stag (which we had not noticed) sprang to his feet, anxious to retain his harem. Because he was not immediately aware of us, he bleated as he pursued a hind. The stag actually managed to turn her back – for a short time.

The evacuation of the area continued. Deer melted into the

woodland, and some half-hearted stag roaring was heard. We were left in the company of the forlorn young stag.

A powerful roaring made the air tremble. The sound reverberated. A stag who was evidently larger than the one seen with the hinds was now announcing his presence. We went slowly uphill to investigate.

The stag was a royal and its antlers were massive, widespreading. He had a very light face. The roaring stopped, but he stood long enough for us to take in his form and features before moving silently away, down the slope, beside a rough scree, going out of sight behind the many trees. We found, nearby, the stub of an antler that had worked its way up through the leaf mould. Cast antlers do not remain for long; they are chewed up when the deer crave for calcium.

A stag that retires after a spell with the hinds is said to be run out. If he is allowed a period of recuperation on good pasture-land, he soon regains his fitness. But if the weather 'closes in' – if winter comes early – the stag might be in no condition to withstand the rigours; he dies.

The hills become littered with deer corpses. The flesh is taken by scavengers such as the fox, golden eagle, raven, buzzard and hooded crow. Some substances are absorbed by the ground.

One deer-watcher advises landowners to leave deer corpses where they are, adding: "Let nature re-cycle them!"

20

Creatures at Dusk

As darkness came, a roe doe and her offspring appeared at the edge of the big wood. The doe used her early-warning devices, acute hearing and smell, to assure herself that the sounds and scents in the air offered no threat to her. The deer moved out confidently to graze.

In one of several vigils at dusk, I hoped to watch the roe until total darkness, when I always yearn to possess some infra-red binoculars, if such a marvel exists. We have to base our knowledge of animals almost entirely on daytime sightings.

The pleasure of watching what I consider to be the most graceful of our native deer was offset by a hubbub in the shrubby understorey of the big wood, more precisely a clump of shrubs at one end. A steady twittering was detectable.

So persistent was the clamour, I left the roe and worked my way round the wood. The few birds that continued to fly were thrush-like. One of the soloists was undoubtedly a blackbird, but which species was represented in the chorus line?

The shrubs were mainly rhododendrons – quite young trees, not yet at the 'leggy' stage when the branches extend far out like the framework of a tent. The waxy leaves hid the birds from my sight. Three thrushes alighted on a birch tree; they moved and called excitedly, and now that I had something on which to focus my binoculars I rapidly identified them. It was easy. Each bird had a prominent white stripe above the eye. I was watching redwings, immigrants from the forests of Scandinavia and western Russia. They are among the most typical birds of a Scottish autumn.

An old chap I met called the redwings, and their close cousins the fieldfares, 'snow thrushes'. They do not arrive with snow on their feet, but their presence gives a broad hint that the year is declining fast.

159

Redwings are restless; they move about the countryside at the dictates of food and weather, so that birds caught and 'ringed' in Britain one winter might turn up in continental Europe, as far away as Italy, some twelve months later.

In autumn, I listen for the flight call – a sibilant *see-ip, see-ip*. In calm weather, redwings arrive at their roost early, and an hour or so may be spent in carefree flights or choral activity. A friend in north-west England has seen a roost containing over 1,000 birds. He told me that blackbirds (also, surprisingly, finches) share the same shrubbery at nightfall. One snowy night, he trudged through snow in a city park and found redwings roosting in shrubbery. He was able to lift some of the birds from the branches.

Look for the redwing by day where trees hold a scarlet film – the effect of massed berries. When the main banquet of berries is over, the redwing inspects the ground beneath the trees, and then it takes to the open, frequently feeding in the company of other thrushes.

The late Ralph Chislett was fascinated by fieldfares. Occasionally, he heard a song from one of the last birds to leave this country in spring for the return to the nesting grounds. He also followed the redwing to Swedish Lapland and afterwards wrote of its haunts in birch woods "growing on the low hillsides, impinging on the great marshes or along the rocky shore of Tornetrask, above which gleamed the snows of the high fjeld".

Chislett described the song he heard in Britain as a "richly throated and fluty song, repeated several times in descending tones". At the Scandinavian nesting grounds, the song ended with a low warble. I have heard the song, but not the warble, in northern Scotland. Of recent years, a few redwing pairs have stayed behind to nest.

The redwing could find many suitable nesting areas in the Highlands. In the north lands, the birds nest in areas that are lightly wooded, and where the dominant trees are birch, willow and alder. The nest is usually low down on a tree, sometimes not much more than a foot from the ground.

Redwings arriving in Britain in October dally through the long winter and often stay until well into our spring. For it is usually June before their Scandinavian nesting programme can get under way. From which area had. the redwings in the shrubbery come? Some of the refugees from the far northern winter that settle happily in Scotland have nested in western Russia.

A familiar sight at dusk is of fieldfares trailing across the sky to their roost. They fly at moderate speed, at moderate height. Sometimes they appear to be lazy, as though they wished to delay the time they must spend in sleep.

The handsome fieldfare is usually more numerous, and more conspicuous, than the redwing. I saw flocks around Loch Lomond and the Trossachs; they flew fairly low, maintaining speed and direction with flicks of their wings. When a flock descended on thorn trees that had not yet been stripped of their berries, the birds were very active and vocal, like small boys at a party.

The call of the fieldfare – a harsh *tchak-tchak* – is distinctive, though it has been compared to the call of the magpie. In the field, look for the bird's grey patches – grey on the head and rump. A pale blue-grey, it contrasts with the chestnut of the bird's back and its very dark tail. Parties of fieldfares, in streamer-like formations, seem to let the wind carry them where it will. In small glens that are scarlet-tinged with berries, the *tchak* of the fieldfare may be the dominant sound for days as the birds exhaust the food supply.

The fieldfare is colonial at nesting time. Find one nest, and you may find a score. The Swedes call it 'birch thrush', and it is a typical bird of the northern birch forests. Visitors to Lapland in June commented on the pugnacity of the birds. The humans were dived on by birds that displayed something of the fearless verve of big gulls at a coastal nesting colony.

The fieldfare, like the redwing, is now a Scottish nesting species. So the 'snow thrushes' – and sometimes the snow itself – are with us the whole year through.

As the sun sets, and humans settle themselves comfortably indoors, our 'little British bear' goes his rounds. The badger leaves his sett in the gloom. He likes to be back underground by dawn.

Knowing that autumn is the season when a badger lays on fat, I used to picture him gorging so as to provide a reserve of nourishment on which he might draw during stormy winter days when he could be restricted to the sett for days on end.

A friend who has kept a boar badger for nine years found by experience just how much food to give his charge to keep him healthy. He does not vary the ration of food from day to day, month after month, though in due course the badger itself declines the full portions, becomes lethargic and eventually stops feeding. His appetite rallies at the close of winter. This badger at least does not gorge in autumn.

A sow badger is mated in February, and in autumn there are fertilized eggs within her. They do not become implanted in the uterine wall until the end of the year, and the young develop rapidly; they are born about two months later.

It was at dusk – a magical time for badgers and badger-watchers – that I last saw the captive animal. The owner shouted his name. Moments later I saw the black and white of a badger's head appear at the sett's entrance. Incidentally, the sett is made of breeze blocks and the badger's yard is covered with a layer of concrete, but the man allows the badger the freedom of the garden for limited periods in the evening.

The animal I saw had all the alertness of a wild badger. He stood, unmoving, for minutes on end. Only the head was visible. The man called again. Out came the squat little badger, and he lumbered across the enclosure on short legs, his body a mass of coarse grey hairs – the type of hairs which used to form the 'business end' of shaving brushes, also sporrans!

The badger's first task was to 'set scent'. He walked to the man, turning at the final approach. The badger lifted his tail, backed against the man's left shoe and squirted liquid from the musk gland as a mark of recognition and also, I suppose, as a mark of proprietorship in the area. Far from being displeased, the man fondled the badger's head.

He then showed me the scar of a nasty wound he had received from his pet. The jaws of a badger have enormous power and, indeed, when an animal has died and the tissue has gone the jaws are seen to remain attached to the skull.

The man provided some clean straw; he simply dumped this material in the yard, and I watched the badger quickly make a bundle of straw. Holding that bundle between his chest, chin and forelegs, the animal shuffled backwards into the hole. I was invited to put my hand inside the sett. It was as hot as an oven.

The badger population in the Highlands – where, incidentally, animals are said to be larger than those of the Lowlands – is rallying after years of persecution. There are more badgers in more places. A forester who was deep-ploughing a hill before tree-planting took place mentioned his surprise when he saw that the blade had sliced through the entry to a badger sett. He was impressed by the speed at which the occupants patched up their home during the night.

A natural sett is not simply a burrow leading to a chamber but a system of chambers, linked by tunnels, some of which extend to the surface. It is invariably established on a slope, an aid to excavation; its also permits efficient drainage.

Visitors to wildlife parks where badgers are accommodated are being invited to see the animals below ground, during the day. Visitors enter lightproof huts and peer through plate glass at the sleeping badgers. I recall visiting a forest park in Speyside where I climbed up some wooden steps and looked into a fenced-off enclosure. The captive badger had had its normal pattern of life — sleeping by day, foraging by night – disturbed for the benefit of humans. It was being fed out of doors during the visiting period!

In autumn, when the vegetation is dying off and there is crisp, dry bracken near at hand, the badger drags in quantities of bedding; he is preparing his sleeping chamber that will serve him in winter, and she (the sow badger) has in mind a comfortable nursery chamber for the cubs. Bedding can be hard to come by in midwinter, so badgers take advantage of dry spells to bring out the old bedding to dry.

A watcher of wild badgers must move silently, always into the wind. I prefer to use a convenient tree as a perch. A forked branch can be made comfortable for a long vigil, and high above the ground my scent is carried well above the badger's head. I walk up to the sett itself at the start of a series of watches to assure myself it is actually being used. One evening I stared at a hole until my eyes prickled; next day, visiting the hole, I found it was draped with cobwebs!

Signs of habitation are clear to see. The entrance to the sett is firm and smooth, often with badger prints on the earth outside. I look for the latrines, in which there may be fresh dung. Trees may have been vertically scratched by a badger that reared up on its hind legs.

Spring days are memorable for the entertainment provided by other birds and beasts during the long watch before a badger appears. At one sett, I used a tree perch and saw a woodcock fly by, night after night. The bird was moving some 50 feet above the ground, which meant that it was passing the tree not very far above my head. On still evenings, the roding wood-cock's call – three grunts and a squeak – was the loudest sound in the wood.

I recall evenings in May, when the sow led her cubs into the world. The cubs ran about the area, noisily fought with each other, playfully nipped the ears of mother, and for ever squeaked with excitement. The boar would usually leave his mate and offspring and wander off! In autumn, as the bracken died back, I saw more of the badgers than I had done in summer. Acorns seemed a popular item on their menu. A nest of wild bees was ransacked for honey.

A dedicated badger-watcher feels his scalp prickling with excitement when the animal first reveals itself. A head appears at the sett's capacious mouth; the black-and-white striped pattern makes it clear to see. For a while the badger stands, listening, tasting the air, doubtless also looking about. The head moves from side to side and also up and down.

A first task on emerging is to indulge in a round of ecstatic scratching and grooming. The badger, though a clean animal in its ways, inevitably picks up lice and fleas. The discomfort is alleviated as the claws rake through the wiry grey coat. I have seen badgers lying on the base of their backs and scratching their bellies. It must be distressing to such an animal when a foul-smelling fox family takes up residence in part of the sett. A fox bringing food to its cubs may leave around the area the remains of its prey. Many badgers are blamed for the fox's crimes against lambs and chickens.

Wherever badger-watchers meet, stories are told of im-probable happenings. I heard of a man who took a small group of people to a favourite complex of setts in an oakwood. One of the wives was excitable and noisy, and so she was allocated a hole up the hillside, where she was away from the others. No one told her that the hole had not been used by badgers for months! The vigil began. Chuckles of delight came from this woman. The others, looking towards her, saw that a badger had appeared and she was feeding it with a biscuit!

A photographer decided to use flash-powder near a badger sett. Because the evening was damp he covered the powder with a plastic bag. A helpful wind wafted his face as he lay a few yards from the mouth of a sett. The badger trundled into view. He released the camera shutter and ignited the flash powder. There was such a flash that for ages afterwards he could see only a display of purple flashes. But he recalled the departure of the badger. The animal must also have been startled by the flash and, the photographer claims, had difficulty in locating the mouth of the sett through which it might dash to the safety of the underworld!

Badger-watchers are among the most dedicated of naturalists. They visit the setts throughout the year, for a badger does not hibernate; it is simply less active in winter.

It is one of many creatures to be seen in the Highlands at dusk.

21

Destination Callander

You may recall that we left Dorothy Wordsworth contemplating a few "Scotch fir" by the Black Mount. The note-taking of this observant woman was not restricted to features of the natural scene; she also took a lively interest in the life of Highland folk.

Especially in the matter of food.

A Highland breakfast today is so nourishing it takes a full day for a person's ribs to settle back into place. At times, Dorothy and William Wordsworth suffered indifferent meals at inns and cottages.

Before crossing the Black Mount, they stayed at Kingshouse. The peats on the fire were wet; they smouldered rather than burned. Dorothy, rising at 6 a.m., requested two boiled eggs for their breakfast. She must have caught the staff napping. A small boy was sent to the outbuildings for eggs, and he found only one egg. The travellers resumed their wanderings stiff with cold and, doubtless, suffering from hunger-knock.

A poor breakfast followed at the inn of Inveroran, but Dorothy forgot her hunger as she looked round the kitchen. Peering through the smoke of a peat fire, she saw drovers and their dogs. Each drover dined on porridge, which had been supplied to him in a wooden bowl. The Wordsworths remembered another hostelry because the servant was surly. It seems that she expected them to order wine, and was disappointed when they did without it.

Peat fires continued to flavour Highland homes for many years. I remember a peat fire for the time it took for the turves to emit heat, and for the fine white dust deposited on the furniture. T. Ratcliffe Barnett, who wrote *The Road to Rannoch* (1924), remembered, during a visit to the Bridge of Orchy, "a whiff of peat-reek from the kitchen fires". A mere handful of houses cluster near the bridge, and Barnett also noted a breath of resin from the little pines, salmon in the river, red deer on the hill, a shop, a post office and a policeman. "And what more could any reasonable man wish for?"

I drove into Crianlarich under the stern gaze of Ben More. The village lies in a basin, ringed by hills. The strong tones of autumn gave the impression that the district was smouldering. Bracken tinted the slopes. Native deciduous trees stood with arms full of colourful leaves.

Here, about half-way between Glasgow and Fort William, the old West Highland Railway established a staging post. A locomotive, hot and bothered after the run up Glen Falloch, was watered. The passengers, by now dry of mouth, could buy some refreshments. The speciality in the old days was food provided in baskets, a custom that minimized the time taken to order a meal.

The modern diesel makes light of the journey but is, in any case, restricted in speed to 40 miles an hour. The line has an aversion to going straight for long. Some of the curves are impressively tight.

The Wordsworths had decided to visit Callander and the Trossachs but they prolonged their Highland jaunt by following the valley of the Tay, by way of Killin and Kenmore. So did I, and at Killin I saw water foaming against boulders and signs reminding me that Ben Lawers was near. This calcareous mountain, which touches the clouds at 3,984 feet, is now the property of the National Trust for Scotland. I had an overwhelming desire to climb high and see the crinkled leaves of cloudberry, a plant that keeps its head down to avoid the worst of the weather.

From the Ben I looked down on Loch Tay, which is 20 miles long and has a higher rainfall at the western end than is recorded at the east. I walked through one of the celebrated oakwoods as a breeze half-filled the air with spinning leaves and a party of assorted titmice examined the trees for food. Macgillivray, a fine naturalist, wrote in 1840 that ospreys were to be seen at Loch Tay.

I was in bbreadalbane country. He who presided over the estate in 1769 (which was the year Thomas Pennant toured the area) had a road made on the northern side of the loch at his own expense. His masons had constructed "thirty-two stone bridges over the torrents that rush from the mountains into the lake". The benevolent Breadalbane also distributed spinning wheels among his tenants, who had previously spun using dangling rocks. Pennant watched people spinning in this way as they tended the cattle on the hills. (At Dent, on the Pennines, farming folk hand-knitted as they supervised their livestock.)

Pennant studied the game of the hillsides. He wrote of a "peculiar species of hare which is found on the summits of the highest hills and never mixed with the common kind which is frequent enough in the vale". This was the blue, white, mountain or variable hare – take your pick of name – that from October to December assumes a white coat, a process triggered off by decreasing daylight. White hair grows through the brown pelage of early autumn and eventually replaces it. (In fact, it has been found that only 1 per cent of Scottish hares go completely white; the black tips to the ears are retained the whole year through.)

Swarms of mountain hares tenant the Perthshire hills, from about 1,000 to 2,500 feet above sea level. I have mentioned that one Easter I motored from Kenmore along a road that had just been opened to traffic and, crossing the moors as the day ended, I watched hares (several hundred were in view) settle down to graze; the species feeds mainly at night.

Recent winters had been mild. The hares on that moorland stood out from the dark ground like cobs of lime in a meadow. I counted so many hares I wearied of this unprofitable game and settled down to watch the animals. I braked the car. A few hares, instantly alert, reared up on their hind legs, their forelegs dangling; the hares peered at me with unblinking eyes. Their ears – which are shortish compared to those of the brown hare of the Lowlands – turned like sensitive radar scanners.

This autumn, I ignored the high road from Kenmore and returned by Loch Tay, eventually driving into Callander – the Tannochbrae of a famous television series about the doings of a grumpy old Highland doctor, his young partner and their redoubtable housekeeper. At Callander, many of the trees were so autumnally bright they might have been on fire.

I have mentioned the writings of T. Ratcliffe Barnett. Our author visited the Trossachs when the craze for owning cars was not yet a problem, and suddenly exclaimed: "Blessed be petrol, which can whisk us so suddenly from all the teasing noises of a town into their fairy solitude [Loch Katrine] with the blue smoke of the fire rising from the heather knoll into the still air. The workmen are busy at the new road which is to raise the level of Loch Katrine for the third time. How time passes!"

What is a Trossach? A man I saw near Aberfoyle kept his face straight, but could not banish the twinkle from his eyes, as he replied to this question. "A Trossach?" he said, echoing my words. "Well, now, I'm glad you asked me that! It's a shy wee creature. About the size of a rabbit, but covered with black fur. Rather cuddly. You'll sometimes see one running across the road a little ahead of the car."

I did not interrupt.

"A Trossach hibernates in winter. It can't find enough food then. For it lives by going through litter bins. Apple cores. Bits of orange peel. A few pieces of potato crisps left in the bottom of a bag. So, you see, it's dependent on the tourist trade."

He exploded with laughter, and handed me a brightly pro-duced leaflet about the Trossachs. It made no mention of such a creature. The Trossachs means, literally, 'The Bristly Place'. The name is singular, not plural as one would expect.

Strictly speaking – and after my encounter with the romantic Scotsman it was a pleasant change to be serious – the name applies only "to the narrow, tree-filled gorge between Loch Achray and Loch Katrine, in the south-west corner of Perth-shire".

The leaflet writer began to warm to the theme. The Trossachs area is a generic name given to "the whole of that lovely 'Scottish Lake District' which includes Lochs Katrine, Achray and Venachar, surrounded by beautiful mountains, tree-clad on their lower slopes, and Loch Ard, west of Aberfoyle".

I have trained myself, with effort, not to use the words 'lovely' and 'beautiful'. Yet they can be applied to the Trossachs – a quiet, gentle, highly tinted landscape, deeply satisfying in its own way and the type of which a million picture postcards are born.

I turned to the official handbook of the Queen Elizabeth Forest Park and read that the word 'Trossachs' is from *Na trasdaichean*, meaning a transverse glen joining two others.

I was in Scottsland – the district projected as a land of romance by that master story-teller Sir Walter Scott. His popularity among ordinary holidaymakers is assured as long as the SS *Sir Walter Scott* sails on Loch Katrine. Words written by Walter Scott brought the first crowds of eager tourists to the Trossachs.

They had read in *The Lady of the Lake:*

> One burnished sheet of living gold,
> Loch Katrine lay beneath him rolled,
> In all her length far winding lay,
> With promontory, creek and bay,
> And islands that, empurpled bright,
> Floated amid the livelier light,
> And mountains, that like giants stand,
> To sentinel enchanted land.

Less than half a century after those words were penned, a German poet named Theodor Fontane discovered that, already, the magic of the area was potent. And his first question related to the name. What exactly *are* the Trossachs? he demanded. He promptly gave his readers an answer that satisfied him: "They are a pass, a gorge, a hollow way that stretches out beside a little river between the two masses of rock, those of Ben A'an and Ben Venue, which stand like watchmen next to Loch Katrine with their broad backs stretched to Lock Achray. . . ."

Theodor peered at Ben Venue. "The height of this mountain wall is very remarkable," he began, unremarkably, "and the rich forests which grace it up to its highest point contribute not a little to the beauty of the picture. There is layer upon layer of differing vegetation, and while birch trees and aspen almost cover the gorge, there greets us from the centre of the mountain an oak forest above whose verdant crowns black pine trees begin to shoot up, covering the rest of the mountainside up to its peak. . ."

How perceptive, though: that a poet should put into a single, sublime sentence not only the chief glories of the Trossachs –

the soaring rock and many trees – but also, with a naturalist's vision, he should perceive how soil and elevation have led to several distinctive belts of vegetation.

Midway through the nineteenth century, guidebook writers began to stress those aspects of local lore that were made colourful and appealing by Walter Scott. There was a steamer to enable them to explore Loch Katrine without effort – and certainly without getting their feet muddy and wet.

Theodor Fontane clambered aboard the steamer at what he called the least romantic hour of the world ("two o' clock in the afternoon and everybody hungry"). He saw Ellen Island, "at the very beginning of the lake". Then he noted, rather sadly, that "at the moment when we have left Ellen Island behind us, it is all up with our interest in Lock Katrine. The voyage across this much-sung lake is like a dinner that begins with champagne and, after a great deal of dallying over plain claret, ends up with sugar-water".

Everybody and everything was called MacGregor. "The bare-legged boy who presses his services as a guide upon us, the two old men who carry our luggage on to the steamer, and needless to say the steamer itself. But a certain amount of rather obvious intention, a certain amount of speculation on the Southrons' thirst for the Highlands, is something that one can put up with in such a spot as this."

We have generally followed the Wordsworthian route. In 1803, they sampled the Trossachs from west to east, however, crossing Loch Lomond by boat to Inversnaid, and then striding on to Glen Gyle and Loch Katrine. A boat journey down the loch brought them to the Trossachs, where they scanned Ben Venue and Loch Achray.

Dorothy commented on the luxuriance of the heather. It is luxuriant today wherever the area has not received a spruce blanket. She noticed that the heather was so tall "that a child of ten years old struggling through it would often have been buried head and shoulders, and the exquisite beauty of the colour, near or at a distance, seen under the trees, is not to be conceived . . ."

Scottish mist blunted the landscape. They could not see the full length of Katrine, but perceived that "it was a gentle place, with lovely open bays, one small island, cornfields, woods and a group of cottages". Rain fell as the party voyaged back up the loch; they lodged at the ferryman's house and next day they crossed over to Inversnaid.

Back in September, after their West Highland tour, they reached Callander and then journeyed westwards by Loch Venachar to the road's ending at the head of Loch Achray. And they took to their feet to explore the area around Loch Katrine, trudging on its northern shore and spending a night at the ferryman's house.

This would have been more than enough for the average visitor, but the Wordsworths went across to Loch Lomond, which they crossed by boat; they penetrated the wooded fast-nesses of Falloch before swinging back to the head of Katrine. The boatman took them back to their starting point. They walked again on the two succeeding days – northwards from Katrine, round to Callander where, let it be whispered in the presence of indolent holidaymakers, they arrived in time to have breakfast!

Sir Walter Scott, who knew the Trossachs well, travelled on horseback. He harked back to what was fondly thought of as the romantic age, peopling the area with kings and courtiers but being nonetheless perceptive when viewing the countryside. In one of his most rousing tales, *Rob Roy*, he eventually began to portray the lives of quite ordinary people . . .

However, the words of Scott that applied most strongly to my evening jaunt from Callander described a lively stag hunt:

> Few were the stragglers, following far,
> That reached the lake of Vennachar;
> And when the Brigg of Turk was won,
> The headmost horseman rode alone.

Venachar, 'the pointed loch', had stands of conifers but also, on the rocks at the edge of the road, some common ling that had become shrub-like in size because it was unvisited by sheep. At the Brig o' Turk I was the last customer of the day at tea rooms where hot tea, scones, butter and jam were served in delightfully old-fashioned ways: old-fashioned in the sense that one did not queue at a self-service counter and receive food on

plastic plates. I asked about the name Turk; it is derived from a
name for the wild boar.

I saw a Scots pine with a monkey-puzzle tree as its neighbour.
Then into view came the Trossachs Hotel, cliff-like in scale,
with spired turrets in the Walter Scott style. The road to Loch
Katrine ran between oakwoods and ended with a flourish in an
enormous car park (admission 10p). The first of many notices
confronted me. A sign requested visitors not to throw coins in
the loch, an idea that would not have occurred to me.

The SS *Sir Walter Scott* was tethered to a wooden pier; all
was in shadow, for Ben Venue seemed to block out half the
sky. The name means 'hill of the young cattle', and years ago a
host of cattle would have trampled down the bracken and
copiously manured the ground.

The Wordsworths looked at this high hill on a day when its
top was concealed by cloud. They noticed that its side, rising
directly from the lake, was covered with birch trees to a great
height, "and seamed with innumerable channels of torrents".

Let Dorothy provide a word-picture of the hill:

> Above and below us, to the right and to the left, were rocks, knolls,
> and hills, which, wherever anything could grow – and that was
> everywhere between the rocks – were covered with trees and
> heather; the trees did not in any place grow so thick as ordinary
> wood; yet I think there was never a bare space of twenty yards: it
> was more like a natural forest where trees grow in groups or
> singly, not hiding the surface of the ground, which, instead of
> being green and mossy, was of the richest purple.

The Wordsworths lived at a time when in their beloved Lake
District, and in the parts of Scotland to which they became
attached, the works of man had not yet begun to dominate the
works of nature. There was still a fine harmony of rocks and
trees, sky and water. A stranger at Loch Katrine today is in no
doubt that this is a reservoir. The Wordsworths were rowed
down Katrine when it was truly a loch, and a little out-of-the-
way.

I saw a promenade, white railings and a tidemark around the
base of knolls that were dominated by pine, of which the
prolific Sir Walter wrote:

And, higher yet, the pine-tree hung
His shattered trunk, and frequent flung
   Where seem'd the cliffs to meet on high,
   His boughs athwart the narrow'd sky.

These were Katrine's pines; the quotation comes from *The Lady of the Lake.*

Katrine has paid for its popularity. The water authorities have undoubtedly done their best to accommodate the visitors. Yet the number of tourists has been impossibly high, not just here but in many parts of Britain, including the Lake District. Stretches of water have become reservoirs, and the ground has been beaten to a concrete hardness.

I followed the broad, hard path beside Loch Katrine, and noticed with joy that wild Scotland was asserting itself at the very edge. On one side were railings, beyond which the water smacked its lips against rocks; on the other side I beheld a tangle of Highland vegetation in which were represented ling, bell heather, also blackberries and some wild sage. Rowans enlivened the craggy areas.

Hearing the shriek of a jay, I sucked the back of my hand – a process known to some naturalists as 'kissing the jay' – hoping to draw a bird towards me by imitating one of its calls. The sound must have been unconvincing – or perhaps it was the wrong time of the year!

The railings were adorned by spiders' webs, which had lost their effectiveness as collectors of flies. The autumn wind had plucked a mass of seed from rosebay willow herb and had blown the seed against the gossamer. The webs resembled pieces of cotton wool.

22

A Forest Never Sleeps

The Forestry Commission had just planted its millionth acre in Scotland, where it employs over 3,000 men.

The sitka spruce is at the top of the forester's list of desirable trees, and about 400 million have been rooted in Britain. They stand like battalions of troops clad in dark green battledress. Their name comes from that of a district on an island lying off Alaska.

Fifty years ago, many of the conifers that now grow in their tens of thousands were listed in the books of British Sylviculture as 'exotics' – if they were mentioned at all. The lodgepole pine, now commonly seen in Scotland, was named from the use that Red Indians made of its trunk for their lodges. Noble fir is a handsome stranger from the Pacific seaboard.

Douglas fir, another North American species, should feel at home in Scotland if only because it was named after a Scot, David Douglas, a native of Perthshire; he sent the first seeds to Europe in the 1820s. Justice was done to Archibald Menzies, another Scot who had collected specimens of the tree some thirty years before, when his name was incorporated in the scientific name of the species – *Pseudotsuga menziesii*.

The list of tree immigrants from the New World to Scotland continues with Lawson's Cypress, grand fir, Colorado white fir, Californian redwood, western red cedar, western hemlock. It is no longer necessary for the makers of a film about Red Indians to ship the actors and camera crew across the Atlantic. Many an Indian war has been resolved in the spruce forests of Scotland!

These thoughts came to mind as I planned a visit to the Queen Elizabeth Forest Park. It was a relief during that visit to find that the park is big and varied, and that the Forestry Commission encourages the public to use it as a recreational district.

Down in the forest, something stirred. It was a young roe-buck. When I became aware of the deer, it was already staring hard at me and standing only five paces from the dense cover afforded by a young spruce plantation. Even before I could focus my binoculars, the roebuck was bounding away. He stood briefly on a hummock, willing me to move. He darted through a rent in a pliant barrier of spruce branches, entering a plantation that was so dry and dead-looking I could not find a single slot to indicate the buck's line of departure.

I crawled into the plantation for fifty yards, running the risk of having my coat ripped off my back. It was like being in a sterile world. The ground held spent needles on which the sun never shone. In the windless silence, I began to yearn for a wind on my face.

This was the sort of commercial planting that Wordsworth had in mind when he wrote of "vegetable manufactory". He was contemplating larches, following the development of a fashion for planting this alien species in his beloved Lake District.

As I walked in the Forest Park, I found myself lamenting for the past glories of the Highlands, and especially the glory of the Wood of Caledon – those hundreds of square miles of native forest, consisting mainly of Scots pine, that occupied remote glens and ran up the hillsides.

T. B. Lauder described that old forest well. He came to know tracts of it in upper Deeside, around Braemar. His word pictures are worthy of contemplation today.

Lauder walked in the pinewood's gloom, "hardly conscious that the sun is up, save from the fragrant resinous odour which its influence is exhaling, and the continued hum of the clouds of insects that are dancing in its beams over the tops of the trees". He entered a sunlit glade, where Nature "pours forth her richest Highland treasures of purple heathbells, and green bilberries, and trailing whortleberries, with tufts of ferns and tall junipers irregularly intermingled".

He reached the top of a hill, sat on bare rock, looked round and exulted: "The forest is seen stretching away in all directions from our feet, mellowing as it recedes into the farthest valleys amid the distant hills, climbing their bold sides, and scattering off in detachments along their steeps like the light troops of some army skirmishing in the van . . . ."

The Caledonian Pine Forest has shrunk to a dozen or so well-known patches. The quietness within them is that of an old cathedral. The few sounds merely accentuate the silence. I recall the rasping of a squirrel's claws against the trunk of a pine as a Highland red squirrel gained elevation – and safety. There was a warm, dreamy day when I heard the shutter of cone scales from the places where crossbills were feeding.

The Speyside forests – expansive, resinous, carpeted with ling and other berried plants – gave me my introduction to the wooded glory of Old Caledonia. I remember the merry calls of crested tits drifting down from the crowns of Scots pines, the explosive force exerted by a capercaillie as it became airborne, and the roe deer in summer red.

I went on to explore other tracts of pinewood, such as Ballochbuie in Deeside – where Lauder was impelled to write so feelingly – and the dark, drool trees beside Loch Maree. I had already renewed my association with the Black Wood of Rannoch.

The old pine forest endures as a special kind of scenery. Possibly in many years to come the new-style spruce forest will have its praises sung by naturalists, though it is pre-eminently a commercial forest. The trees grow with almost the speed of rhubarb. They are clear-felled in much less than the span of a man's life.

Two modern forests, and part of another, were brought together as the Queen Elizabeth Forest Park of about 65 square miles. The trees are seen in their massed glory only about 20 miles north of Glasgow. In the foreword to the forest guide it is stated: "The area marches with the main part of the beautiful Trossachs. Plantations covering an area of over 32,000 acres have been established, while 10,000 acres of lochs and mountains remain available for those who find joy and recreation in exploring the wild countryside."

Half a dozen of the people I met at Aberfoyle had clear memories of the district as it was before the Coming of the Conifers. Or they quoted tales related by their parents. Their remembrances tended to have about them a golden aura of nostalgia. What they recalled was a mainly pastoral scene, with farmers, cattle, sheep. The trees were of native stuff and – unlike spruce – did not clog the scenery. Aberfoyle's farming background is testified to by the existence until 1890 of an autumn fair at which cattle were purchased and servants hired for another term.

In the 1920s, when the Forestry Commission acquired the first of its many acres between Lomondside and the Menteith Hills, the farmers were in fact struggling against contrary economic forces. Cattle and sheep tended to struggle as well. A report of 1793 described the district as "wet but healthy", yet quite a few sheep grazing the marshy bottoms developed fluky livers.

The Forestry Commission had simply turned back the clock a few centuries and, in its choice of trees, brought in some potentially handsome strangers.

Woodland and farm stock do not go together unless some attempt is made to protect the woodland. Goats were apparently common; they certainly would not allow the woods to regenerate themselves naturally. At one time, oak was planted to be coppiced; it yielded fibre for tanning and other industries. Some measure of stock control was necessary. If you would picture the district as it was in an oakwood stage, then look at Doon Hill near Aberfoyle.

I spent a day in the forest. My walk began at Aberfoyle, the park's largest township. I looked down on the young River Forth, which has its source on rush ground to the north of Ben Lomond. The valley of the Forth was one feature to be viewed from a window at the David Marshall Lodge, in the Forest Park.

The final approach to that lodge was notable for the autumnal beauty of birch and oak, the former appearing to shimmer as a host of golden leaves were strummed by a light breeze. Once there was a commercial demand for birch; it was converted into charcoal to supply the local iron trade. Now the birch prettily adorns the scene – a tree with a fairly short life, for it is a ready prey to fungus. Many birches grow and topple in less than a century.

On the first leg of the walk to Loch Ard, Douglas fir confronted me, and I saw sitka spruce occupying land where the forest had been naturally thinned by a 1968 gale. The spruce roots in a shallow fashion, and the modern forester seeks to lower the water table through drainage to encourage those roots to go deeper.

Foresters have neat and tidy minds; they like to work to a plan. It distresses them when a gale frolics through the district, dropping trees like rows of upreared dominoes, for then a good management scheme can be brought to nought. Time must be spent on tidying up and abstracting timber that was prematurely felled. Sitka spruce goes over, roots and all. Even giant conifers succumb to a gale. One night in 1975, a dozen fine, 70-feet-high Scots pines on a ridge a few miles from my home were toppled. Three of them actually snapped off near the base of the trunk.

The foresters who first worked in the area that has become the Queen Elizabeth Forest Park were accustomed to hand operations. Even drainage channels were dug by hand. Not until the late 1930s did the first of the heavy machines arrive. Now crawler tractors fitted with ploughs trundle across the scene like latter-day dinosaurs. Aircraft occasionally buzz over the plantations and distributes phosphate to correct a mineral deficiency in the soil. Lorries use miles of special forest roads to remove the matured timber.

A forest never sleeps. Even a modern spruce forest gathers around itself a rich and varied wildlife. The largest and grandest of the birds at Queen Elizabeth is the capercaillie, which I had already seen. Now I had the good fortune to observe a young hen bird who had pitched on to the branch of a Scots pine and, in the colourful light of evening, was ripping off needles. The bird looked huge, and the chosen branch was bent out of line by its weight, yet it did not fracture, and the caper made a dozen fine adjustments to her trim to ensure that she could stand there firmly.

I noticed some nests of wood ants – heaps formed of tawny conifer needles. Ants appear on the menu of the capercaillie. A gamekeeper told me that when he reared some orphan young birds he dug into a wood-ant nest to provide them with food. In Grizedale Forest, in north-west England, to which capercaillie were introduced from Scotland, there were no wood-ant nests so whole colonies were moved in from a neighbouring dale.

The capercaillie is a late arrival in a conifer forest. When the land is first planted, larks and pipits continue to inhabit the lush tangle of ground vegetation, and the curlew continues to enliven the spring and summer days with its bubbling song.

Keep out deer and sheep from an area of grassland, and you will be impressed by the speed at which the various species of grass assert themselves. The tousled vegetation makes a perfect home – and provides abundant vegetarian food – for legions of small mammals, especially voles. In what are called 'vole years', when a population reaches its peak, soon to crash again, a vole scurries away from you at every other footfall.

To a peckish owl or hawk, a vole is a fur-wrapped packet of protein. I used to watch birds in a conifer forest where barn owls flew. They were supreme 'mousers', and when a pair responded to the prolonged hunger calls of the young they operated a shuttle-service with voles as food. The luckless mammals were brought to the nest at intervals of a few minutes.

The bird I most readily associate with a conifer forest in its early stages is the short-eared owl. It was a delight to see one at the edge of the Queen Elizabeth Forest Park. In favourable areas, vole numbers fluctuate on a cycle, with a peak about every four years; it has been reported that during one 'vole year' between thirty and forty pairs of short-eared owls bred in about five square miles of new forest.

In autumn, the short-eared owls prepare to leave the nesting areas for lower ground, including the coastal marshes. But the first of the owls return as early as February. I love to see them flying like big brown moths, suddenly making quarter-turns before plunging to the ground to collect small mammals.

The display flight is curious. A bird circles high, and then brings its long wings smartly together beneath its body with that sort of snapping sound heard when wood-pigeons are flushed from a wood. The owl's tattoo involves four or five beats. The bird drops during the performance, but when the wings are spread out again, grace returns to its flighting.

The precocious young of short-eared owls wander anything

up to a hundred yards from the nest. I have seen them staring blandly at me while a parent bird circled high against the blue vault of the sky, rounded wings beating slowly.

If a new forest is established on former agricultural land, and buildings are left standing, the kestrels have ideal nesting places. Their nests are lagged with the fur of many voles. Farmsteads that have been vacated seem to attract black grouse in autumn. They collect at the rowan trees planted by superstitious folk many years ago, the idea being to ward off the harmful effects of witches. Black grouse dine on ripe rowan berries.

When, in due season, the planted trees smother the ground, a walk through the forest is notable for the number of finches that are seen. And an increasing number of goldcrests are heard. Their call, *see, see, see,* is so thin that you need to have good hearing to detect them.

At nesting time, a pair of goldcrests spends nearly a fortnight making the hammock-like nest of such delicate materials as moss, grass, hair and lichen, also cobwebs. The nest is lined with feathers. A goldcrest nest blends with the spruce tree from one of whose branches it hangs. The world of the goldcrest is dark, windless and secluded.

Where you find goldcrests, the cole tit will not be far away. A friend who erected a dozen or two nesting boxes along the edges of plantations found that most boxes were used by cole tits (some boxes held the nests of wasps, which are also common in a conifer forest). The cole tit's long, thin bill probes into conifer needles and cones for insects and grubs.

As the forest develops further, it becomes sombre. Large birds like crows and pigeons can now find nesting places. The Queen Elizabeth Park is on the famous Boundary Fault, and the crow you see here might be a hooded or a carrion, or even a hybrid. Cascades of wood-pigeons are disturbed; the birds smack their leathery wings when first disturbed. Where new plantations are adjacent to well-established woods of oak or birch scrub, then the jay is a prominent and noisy bird.

The mammals of the forest are shy and retiring. I saw a grey squirrel and I walked through a cloud of evil-smelling vapour left by a departing fox, whose dark foil was to be found beside the track.

At Clashmore Loch, which appeals to the naturalist because here the land is open, I looked across a soggy landscape to Ben Lomond. Bog myrtle had rooted near the loch. A hen harrier was beating the bounds for food.

I had leapt a particular burn before I discovered from the local guide book that it is on the line of the Highland Fault. So I repeated the operation, though a little sadly.

That jump carried me from the Highlands into the Lowlands!

Index

Herring, 19, 43-4, 57, 61, 106
Highland Line, 22-4, 27, 182
Highland Tourist Board, 17
Hill-walkers, 141
Hind, white, 123-5
Holly, 27, 94, 98
Horse, 67
Hydro-electricity, 50, 54-5, 141

Ice Age, 24, 142
Inchcailloch, 21-8, 43
Inchconnel, 53
Inchfad, 26
Inch Galbraith, 25
Inchmurrin, 22, 26
Industrial Revolution, 138
Inishail, 53
Innead a' Cheathaich, 118
Inveraray, 14-15, 40-2, 44, 50, 67, 89
Inverawe House, 55
Invergarry, 98
Inverliever, 52
Inveroran, 166
Inversnaid, 171-2
Inveruglas, 22
Iona, 17, 64
Ireland, 24
Iron, pig, 78
—— smelting, 32
Islay, isle of, 11, 1

Jackdaw, 81
Jacobites, 21, 51, 66, 92
James IV of Scotland, 80, 125
Jay, 35-6, 174, 181
Jellyfish, 15, 44
Johnson, Dr, 42

Kenmore, 167-8
Kerrera, 67, 77

Kestrel, 181
Kidnapped, 121
Kilbrandon, 71
Kilchurn, 50-1, 54
Killin, 122, 167
Kilmartin, 70
Kilpatrick Hills, 21
Kinglass, River, 59
Kingshouse, 119, 122, 166
Kinloch, 150
Kinlochetive, 58-9
Kinloch Hourn, 99, 101, 104-5, 108
Kinlochleven, 113
Kinnoull, 11
Kintyre, 14, 17, 45-6, 89
Kippers, Loch Fyne, 43
Knox, John, 42, 122
Knoydart, 100, 107, 109
Kyle of Lochalsh, 18

Ladhar Bheinn, 97, 108, 112
Lady's Rock, The, 89
Lanark, 21
Landseer, Charles, 145
——, Edwin, 88, 126, 145
Lapwing, 122
Larch, 99, 176
Lauder, T. B., 176-7
Leven, River, 23
Leyden, 115
Liever, River, 59
Lime, 40
Lismore, 79
Lochs
   Achray, 169, 171-2
   Awe, 19, 50-7, 67, 76, 133
   Ard, 169, 178
   Creran 79
   Eck, 24
   Etive, 11, 13, 19, 33, 56-8, 63-5, 77-9, 123